15 MINUTE
SPANISH

15 MINUTE
SPANISH
LEARN IN JUST 12 WEEKS

ANA BREMÓN

 Penguin Random House

Senior Editor Angeles Gavira
Project Art Editor Vanessa Marr
DTP Designer John Goldsmid
Production Controller Luca Frassinetti
Publishing Manager Liz Wheeler
Managing Art Editor Philip Ormerod
Publishing Director Jonathan Metcalf
Art Director Bryn Walls

**Language content produced for Dorling
Kindersley by
g-and-w publishing.**

**Produced for Dorling Kindersley by
Schermuly Design Co.**

First published in Great Britain in 2005 by
Dorling Kindersley Limited
80 Strand, London WC2R 0RL
Penguin Group (UK)

6 8 10 9 7 5
012-HD026-May/2013-book
187521-Jan/13-pack

A CIP catalogue record is available for this book
from the British Library.
ISBN 978-1-4093-7758-0

15-Minute Spanish is available as a book on its own,
in an audio pack with two CDs, or as part of a
complete language pack.

Printed and bound in China

A WORLD OF IDEAS:
SEE ALL THERE IS TO KNOW
www.dk.com

CONTENTS

How to use this book

The main part of the book is devoted to 12 themed chapters, broken down into five 15-minute daily lessons, the last of which is a revision lesson. So, in just 12 weeks you will have completed the course. A concluding reference section contains a menu guide and English-to-Spanish and Spanish-to-English dictionaries.

Warm up
Each day starts with a one-minute warm up that encourages you to recall vocabulary or phrases you have learned previously. To the right of the heading bar you will see how long you need to spend on each exercise.

Instructions
Each exercise is numbered and introduced by instructions that explain what to do. In some cases additional information is given about the language point being covered.

Cultural/Conversational tip
These panels provide additional insights into life in Spain and language usage.

Text styles
Distinctive text styles differentiate Spanish and English, and the pronunciation guide (see right).

In conversation
Illustrated dialogues reflecting how vocabulary and phrases are used in everyday situations appear throughout the book.

How to use the flap
The book's cover flaps allow you to conceal the Spanish so that you can test whether you have remembered correctly.

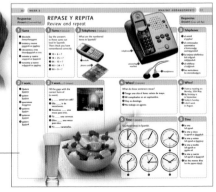

Revision pages
A recap of selected elements of previous lessons helps to reinforce your knowledge.

Useful phrases
Selected phrases relevant to the topic help you speak and understand.

EATING AND DRINKING | 19

4 Useful phrases (5 minutes)

Learn these phrases. Read the English under the pictures and say the phrase in Spanish as shown on the right. Then cover the Spanish with the cover flap and test yourself.

el azúcar
el ah-thookar
sugar

Me pone un café.
may ponay oon kafay

I'll have a black coffee.

¿Eso es todo?
esoh es todoh

Is that all?

Yo voy a tomar churros.
yoh boy ah tomar choorros

I'm going to have some churros.

el café con leche
el kafay kon lechay
white coffee

¿Cuánto es?
kwantoh es

How much is that?

Gracias. ¿Cuánto es?
grathyas. kwantoh es

Thank you. How much is this?

Cuatro euros, por favor.
kwatroh eh-ooros, por fabor

Four euros, please.

Say it
In these exercises you are asked to apply what you have learned using different vocabulary.

6 Say it (2 minutes)

Do you go near the train station?

Do you go near the Prado?

When is the next bus to Barcelona?

Menu guide
Use this guide as a reference for food terminology and popular Spanish dishes.

Pronunciation guide

This book teaches European Spanish, which differs in pronunciation from the various dialects spoken in Latin America. A few Spanish sounds require special explanation:

c a Spanish c is pronounced *th* before i or e but k before other vowels: **cinco** theenkoh (*five*)

h h is always silent: **hola** o-lah (*hello*)

j (g) a Spanish j (and g before i or e) is pronounced as a strong *h*, as if saying *hat* emphasizing the first letter

ll pronounced *y* as in *yes*

ñ pronounced *ny* like the sound in the middle of *canyon*

r a Spanish r is trilled like a Scottish r, especially at the beginning of a word and when doubled

v a Spanish v is halfway between an English *b* and *v*

z a Spanish z is pronounced *th*

Spanish vowels tend to be pronounced shorter than their English equivalents:

a as the English *father*

e as the English *wet*

i as the English *keep*

o as the English *boat*

u as the English *boot*

After each word or phrase you will find a pronunciation transcription, with underlining showing the stress. Remember that this can only be an approximation; there is no substitute for listening to and mimicking native speakers.

Dictionary
A mini-dictionary provides ready reference from English to Spanish and Spanish to English for 2,500 words.

146 DICTIONARY

DICTIONARY
Spanish to English

128 MENU GUIDE

MENU GUIDE
This guide lists the most common terms you may encounter on Spanish menus or when shopping for food. If you can't find an exact phrase, try looking up its component parts.

1 **Warm up** (1 minute)

The Warm Up appears at the beginning of each lesson. It will remind you of what you have already learned and prepare you for moving ahead with the new subject.

HOLA
Hello

In Spain women often greet with one or two kisses on the cheek and men shake other men's hands, although men may kiss or embrace younger male relatives or close friends. In more formal situations – among strangers or in a business context – a handshake is the norm.

¡Hola!
o-lah
Hello!

2 **Words to remember** (2 minutes)

Look at these greetings and say them aloud. Conceal the text on the left with the cover flap and try to remember the Spanish for each item. Check your answers.

Buenos días. *bwenos deeyas*	Good morning/day.
Me llamo Ana. *may yamoh anna*	My name is Ana.
Encantado/-a. *enkan-tadoh/-ah*	Pleased to meet you (man/woman speaking).
Buenas tardes (noches). *bwenas tardes (noches)*	Good afternoon/evening (night).

Cultural tip The Spanish frequently address people as **señor** (*sir*), **señora** (*madam*, for older women), and **señorita** (*miss*, for young women). With first names use **Don** for men or **Doña** for women: **Don Juan**, **Doña Ana**.

3 **In conversation: formal** (3 minutes)

Buenos días. Me llamo Concha García.
bwenos deeyas. may yamoh konchah garthee-ah

Good day. My name's Concha García.

Señor López, encantado.
senyor lopeth, enkan-tadoh

Mr López, pleased to meet you.

Encantada.
enkan-tadah

Pleased to meet you.

4 Put into practice (3 minutes)

Join in this conversation. Read the Spanish beside the pictures on the left and then follow the instructions to make your reply. Then test yourself by concealing the answers on the right with the cover flap.

Buenas tardes señor.
bwenas tardes senyor

Good evening, sir.

Say: Good evening, madam.

Buenas tardes señora.
bwenas tardes senyorah

Me llamo Julia.
may yamoh hoolya

My name is Julia.

Say: Pleased to meet you.

Encantado.
enkan-tadoh

5 Useful phrases (3 minutes)

Read these phrases aloud several times and try to memorize them. Conceal the Spanish with the cover flap and test yourself.

What's your name?	**¿Cómo se llama?** _komo seh yamah_
Goodbye.	**Adiós.** _addy-os_
Thank you.	**Gracias.** _grathyas_
See you soon/tomorrow.	**Hasta pronto/mañana.** _astah prontoh/manyanah_

6 In conversation: informal (3 minutes)

Entonces, ¿hasta mañana?
entonthes, astah manyanah

So, see you tomorrow?

Sí, adiós.
see, addy-os

Yes, goodbye.

Adiós. Hasta pronto.
addy-os. astah prontoh

Goodbye. See you soon.

1 Warm up (1 minute)

Say "hello" and "goodbye" in Spanish. (pp.8-9)

Now say "My name is...". (pp.8-9)

Say "sir" and "madam". (pp.8-9)

LAS RELACIONES
Relatives

The Spanish equivalents of *mum* and *dad* are **mamá** and **papá**. The male plural can refer to both sexes, for example - **niños** (*boys* and *children*), **padres** (*fathers* and *parents*), **abuelos** (*grandfathers* and *grandparents*), **tíos** (*uncles* and *aunt* and *uncle*), **hermanos** (*brothers* and *siblings*), and so on.

2 Match and repeat (5 minutes)

Look at the people in this scene and match their numbers with the list at the side. Read the Spanish words aloud. Now, conceal the list with the cover flap and test yourself.

1 **la hermana**
lah airmanah

2 **el abuelo**
el abweloh

3 **el padre**
el pahdray

4 **el hermano**
el airmanoh

5 **la abuela**
lah abwelah

6 **la hija**
lah ee-hah

7 **la madre**
lah mahdray

8 **el hijo**
el ee-hoh

grandfather **2**   **3** father

sister **1**

4 brother

5 grandmother   **6** daughter   **7** mother   **8** son

Conversational tip In Spanish, things as well as people are masculine or feminine - for example, *wine* is masculine (**el vino**) but *milk* is feminine (**la leche**). Use **los** and **las** for masculine and feminine plurals, respectively. For *a/an*, use **un** for masculine and **una** for feminine items.

3 Words to remember: relatives (4 minutes)

el marido
el mareedoh
husband

la mujer
lah moo-hair
wife

Estoy casado/-a.
estoy kasadoh/-ah
I'm married (m/f).

Familiarize yourself with these words. Read them aloud several times and try to memorize them. Conceal the Spanish with the cover flap and test yourself.

father/mother-in-law	**el suegro/la suegra** *el swegroh/lah swegrah*
stepfather	**el padrastro** *el padras-troh*
stepmother	**la madrastra** *lah madras-trah*
children (male/female)	**los niños/las niñas** *los neenyos/las neenyas*
uncle/aunt	**el tío/la tía** *el tee-oh/lah tee-ah*
cousin	**el primo/la prima** *el preemoh/lah preemah*
I have four children.	**Tengo cuatro niños.** *tengoh kwatroh neenyos*
I have two stepdaughters and a stepson.	**Tengo dos hijastras y un hijastro.** *tengoh dos ee-hastras ee oon ee-hastroh*

4 Words to remember: numbers (3 minutes)

Memorize these words and then test yourself using the cover flap.

Careful when you use the number *one*. When you use **uno** in front of a word it changes to **un** or **una**, depending on whether that word is masculine or feminine. For example: **Tengo un hijo** (*I have one son*), **Tengo una hija** (*I have one daughter*).

one	**uno/-a**	*oonoh/-ah*
two	**dos**	*dos*
three	**tres**	*tres*
four	**cuatro**	*kwatroh*
five	**cinco**	*theenkoh*
six	**seis**	*seys*
seven	**siete**	*syetay*
eight	**ocho**	*ochoh*
nine	**nueve**	*nwebay*
ten	**diez**	*dyeth*

5 Say it (2 minute)

I have five sons.

I have three sisters and a brother.

I have two children.

1 **Warm up** (1 minute)

Say the Spanish for as
many members of the
family as you can.
(pp.10-11)

Say "I have two sons".
(pp.10-11)

MI FAMILIA
My family

There are two ways of saying *you* in Spanish, **usted**
for formal situations and **tú** in informal ones. There
is also a formal way of saying *your* - **su** (singular) and
sus (plural): **usted y su mujer** (*you and your wife*),
¿Son ésos sus hijos? (*Are those your sons?*). **Su** and
sus also mean *his* and *her*.

2 **Words to remember** (5 minutes)

Say these words aloud a few times. Conceal the Spanish with the
cover flap and try to remember the Spanish word for each item.

mi *mee*	my (with singular)
mis *mees*	my (with plural)
tu *too*	your (informal with singular)
tus *toos*	your (informal with plural)
su *soo*	your (formal with singular)
sus *soos*	your (formal with plural)
su *soo*	his/her (with singular) their (with singular)
sus *soos*	his/her (with plural) their (with plural)

Éstos son mis padres.
estos son mees pahdres
These are my parents.

3 **In conversation** (4 minutes)

¿Tiene usted niños?
tyenay oosted neenyos

Do you have any children?

Sí, tengo dos hijas.
see, tengoh dos ee-has

Yes, I have two daughters.

**Éstas son mis hijas.
¿Y usted?**
*estas son mees ee-has.
ee oosted*

These are my daughters.
And you?

Conversational tip The Spanish ask a question by simply raising the pitch of the voice at the end of a statement: **¿Quieres un poco de vino?** (*Do you want a little wine?*). Notice the upside-down question mark (**¿**) written at the beginning of the question. You will also see an upside-down exclamation mark, as in **¡Hola!** (*Hello!*).

4 Useful phrases (3 minutes)

Read these phrases aloud several times and try to memorize them. Conceal the Spanish with the cover flap and test yourself.

Do you have any brothers? (formal)	**¿Tiene usted hermanos?** *tyenay oosted airmanos*
Do you have any brothers? (informal)	**¿Tienes hermanos?** *tyenes airmanos*

This is my husband.	**Éste es mi marido.** *estay es mee mareedoh*
That's my wife.	**Ésa es mi mujer.** *esah es mee moo-hair*

Is that your sister? (formal)	**¿Es ésa su hermana?** *es esah soo airmanah*
Is that your sister? (informal)	**¿Es ésa tu hermana?** *es esah too airmanah*

5 Say it (2 minutes)

No, pero tengo un hijastro.
noh, peroh tengoh oon ee-hastroh

No, but I have a stepson.

Do you have any brothers and sisters? (formal)

Do you have any children? (informal)

I have two sisters.

This is my wife, María.

1 Warm up (1 minute)

Say "See you soon".
(pp.8–9)

Say "I am married"
(pp.10–11) and "I have
a wife". (pp.12–13)

SER Y TENER
To be and to have

Two of the most important verbs are **ser** (to be)
and **tener** (to have). Note that there are different
ways of saying *you*, *we*, and *they*, with formal and
informal, singular and plural, and masculine
and feminine forms. Pronouns (*I*, *you*, etc.) are
omitted where the sense is clear.

2 Ser: to be (5 minutes)

Familiarize yourself with **ser** (to be). When you are
confident, practise the sample sentences below.
Note: there is another verb meaning "to be" –
estar, which is discussed on page 49.

yo soy *yoh soy*	I am
tú eres *too eh-res*	you are (informal singular)
usted es *oosted es*	you are (formal singular)
él/ella es *el/eh-yah es*	he/she is
nosotros/-as somos *nosotros/-as somos*	we are (masculine/ feminine)
vosotros/-as sois *bosotros/-as soys*	you are (informal plural, m/f)
ustedes son *oostedes son*	you are (formal plural)
ellos/-as son *eh-yos/-yas son*	they are (masculine/ feminine)

Yo soy inglesa.
yoh soy eenglesah
I'm English.

¿De dónde es usted? *day donday es oosted*	Where are you from?

Es mi hermana. *es mee airmanah*	She is my sister.

Somos españoles. *somos espanyoles*	We're Spanish.

3 Tener: to have (5 minutes)

¿Tiene rosas rojas?
tyenay rosas rohas
Do you have red roses?

Practise **tener** *(to have)* and the sample sentences, then test yourself.

I have	**yo tengo**	*yoh tengoh*
you have (informal singular)	**tú tienes**	*too tyenes*
you have (formal singular)	**usted tiene**	*oosted tyenay*
he/she has	**él/ella tiene**	*el/eh-yah tyenay*
we have (masculine/feminine)	**nosotros/-as tenemos**	*nosotros/-as tenaymos*
you have (informal plural, m/f)	**vosotros/-as teneis**	*bosotros/-as tenays*
you have (formal plural)	**ustedes tienen**	*oostedes tyenen*
they have (masculine/feminine)	**ellos/-as tienen**	*eh-yos/-yas tyenen*

He has a meeting. **Tiene una reunión.**
tyenay oonah re-oonyon

Do you have a mobile phone? **¿Tiene usted móvil?**
tyenay oosted mobeel?

How many brothers and sisters do you have? **¿Cuántos hermanos tiene usted?**
kwantos airmanos tyenay oosted

4 Negatives (4 minutes)

la bicicleta
lah beetheekletah
bicycle

No tengo coche.
noh tengoh kochay
I don't have a car.

It is easy to make sentences negative in Spanish, just put **no** in front of the verb:
No somos americanos *(We're not American).*

I'm not Spanish.	**No soy español.**	*noh soy espanyol*
He's not a vegetarian.	**No es vegetariano.**	*noh es be-hetaryanoh*
We don't have any children.	**No tenemos niños.**	*noh tenaymos neenyos*

Respuestas
Answers (Cover with flap)

REPASE Y REPITA
Review and repeat

❶ How many

❶ **tres**
tres

❷ **nueve**
nwebay

❸ **cuatro**
kwatroh

❹ **dos**
dos

❺ **ocho**
ochoh

❻ **diez**
dyeth

❼ **cinco**
theenkoh

❽ **siete**
syetay

❾ **seis**
seys

❶ How many (2 minutes)

Cover the answers with the flap. Then say these Spanish numbers out loud. Check you have remembered the Spanish correctly.

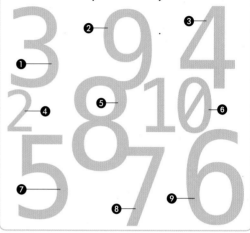

❷ Hello

❶ **Buenos días. Me llamo... [your name].**
bwenos deeyas. may yamoh...

❷ **Encantado/-a.**
enkan-tadoh/-ah

❸ **Sí, y tengo dos hijos. ¿Y usted?**
see, ee tengoh dos ee-hos. ee oosted

❹ **Adiós. Hasta mañana.**
addy-os. astah manyanah

❷ Hello (4 minutes)

You are talking to someone you have just met. Join in the conversation, replying in Spanish following the English prompts.

Buenos días. Me llamo María.
❶ Answer the greeting and give your name.

Éste es mi marido, Juan.
❷ Say "Pleased to meet you".

¿Está usted casado/-a?
❸ Say "Yes, and I have two sons. And you?"

Nosotros tenemos tres hijos.
❹ Say "Goodbye. See you tomorrow".

3 To have or be (5 minutes)

Fill in the blanks with the correct form of **tener** (*to have*) or **ser** (*to be*). Check you have remembered the Spanish correctly.

❶ Yo _____ inglesa.

❷ Nosotros _____ cuatro niños.

❸ Yo no _____ feliz.

❹ ¿ _____ tú coche?

❺ Él _____ mi marido.

❻ Yo no _____ teléfono móvil.

❼ Tú no _____ español.

❽ ¿ _____ usted hijos?

3 To have or be

❶ **soy**
soy

❷ **tenemos**
tenaymos

❸ **soy**
soy

❹ **tienes**
tyenes

❺ **es**
es

❻ **tengo**
tengoh

❼ **eres**
eh-res

❽ **tiene**
tyenay

4 Family (4 minutes)

Say the Spanish for each of the numbered family members. Check you have remembered the Spanish correctly.

grandfather ❷ ❸ father

sister ❶ ❹ brother

❺ grandmother ❻ daughter ❼ mother ❽ son

4 Family

❶ **la hermana**
lah airmanah

❷ **el abuelo**
el abweloh

❸ **el padre**
el pahdray

❹ **el hermano**
el airmanoh

❺ **la abuela**
lah abwelah

❻ **la hija**
lah ee-ha

❼ **la madre**
lah mahdray

❽ **el hijo**
el ee-hoh

EN LA CAFETERÍA
In the café

1 **Warm up** (1 minute)

Count to ten. (pp.10-11)

Remind yourself how to say "hello" and "goodbye". (pp.8-9)

Ask "Do you have a son?" (pp.14-15)

In a Spanish café you can get bread and pastries with your coffee in the mornings. **Churros** (fried dough sticks) are a typical Spanish snack. You can either sit at the counter or have waiter service at a table. It is usual to tip the waiter, but a few coins is usually enough.

el chocolate
el chokolatay
chocolate

2 **Words to remember** (5 minutes)

Familiarize yourself with these words.

el té con limón *el tay kon leemon*	tea with lemon
el café descafeinado *el kafay deskafeynadoh*	decaffeinated coffee
el cortado *el kortadoh*	espresso with a bit of milk
la mermelada *lah mermeladah*	jam
la tostada con mantequilla *lah tostadah kon mantekee-yah*	toast with butter

el café solo
el kafay soloh
espresso

Cultural tip A standard coffee is small and black; if you want it any other way, you'll need to specify. If you want tea with milk, ask for **té con leche**. If you just ask for **té**, you are likely to get tea with lemon.

3 **In conversation** (4 minutes)

Buenos días. Me pone un café con leche.
bwenos deeyas. may ponay oon kafay kon lechay

Hello. I'll have a white coffee, please.

¿Eso es todo?
esoh es todoh

Is that all?

¿Tiene churros?
tyenay choorros

Do you have any churros?

4 **Useful phrases** (5 minutes)

Learn these phrases. Read the English under the pictures and say the phrase in Spanish as shown on the right. Then cover the Spanish with the cover flap and test yourself.

los churros
los <u>choo</u>rros
churros

el azúcar
el ah-<u>thoo</u>kar
sugar

Me pone un café.
may <u>po</u>nay oon ka<u>fay</u>

I'll have a black coffee.

¿Eso es todo?
<u>es</u>oh es <u>to</u>doh

Is that all?

Yo voy a tomar churros.
yoh boy ah to<u>mar</u> <u>choo</u>rros

I'm going to have some churros.

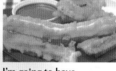

¿Cuánto es?
<u>kwan</u>toh es

How much is that?

el café con leche
el ka<u>fay</u> kon <u>le</u>chay
white coffee

Sí, señor.
see, sen<u>yor</u>

Yes, sir.

Gracias. ¿Cuánto es?
<u>grath</u>yas. <u>kwan</u>toh es

Thank you. How much is that?

Cuatro euros, por favor.
<u>kwa</u>troh eh-<u>oo</u>ros, por <u>fa</u>bor

Four euros, please.

Warm up (1 minute)

Ask "How much is that?"
(pp.18-19)

Say "I don't have a
brother". (pp.14-15)

Ask "Do you have any
churros?" (pp.18-19)

EN EL RESTAURANTE
In the restaurant

There are a variety of different types of eating places
in Spain. In a bar or **tasca** you can find a few **tapas** or
snacks. Lunch is the main meal of the day, but if you are
not very hungry, many restaurants offer **tapas** at the
bar, which is usually very good value for a light meal.

Words to remember (3 minutes)

Memorize these words. Conceal
the Spanish with the cover flap
and test yourself.

la carta *lah kartah*	menu
la carta de vinos *lah kartah day beenos*	wine list
los entrantes *los entrantes*	starters
el plato principal *el platoh preentheepal*	main course
los postres *los postres*	desserts
el desayuno *el desah-yoonoh*	breakfast
el almuerzo *el almooairthoh*	lunch
la cena *lah thenah*	dinner

cup **7**

saucer **8**

5 spoon

6 knife

fork **4**

In conversation (4 minutes)

**Hola. Una mesa para
cuatro, por favor.**
*o-lah. oonah mesah parah
kwatroh, por fabor.*

Hello. A table for
four, please.

¿Tiene una reserva?
tyenay oonah reserbah

Do you have a reservation?

Sí, a nombre de Cortés.
see, ah nombray day kortes

Yes, in the name of Cortés.

4 Match and repeat (4 minutes)

Look at the numbered objects on this table and match them with the items in the vocabulary list at the side. Read the Spanish words aloud. Now, conceal the list with the cover flap and test yourself.

glass ❶

❷ napkin

plate ❸

❶ **la copa**
lah kopah

❷ **la servilleta**
lah serbee-yetah

❸ **el plato**
el platoh

❹ **el tenedor**
el tenedor

❺ **la cuchara**
lah koocharah

❻ **el cuchillo**
el koochee-yoh

❼ **la taza**
lah tathah

❽ **el platillo**
el plateeyoh

5 Useful phrases (4 minutes)

Learn these phrases and then test yourself using the cover flap to conceal the Spanish.

What do you have for dessert?	**¿Qué tiene de postre?** *kay tyenay day postray*
The bill, please.	**La cuenta, por favor.** *lah kwentah, por fabor*

¿Fumadores o no fumadores?
foomadores oh noh foomadores

Smoking or non-smoking?

No fumadores, por favor.
noh foomadores, por fabor

Non-smoking, please.

Síganme, por favor.
seegan-may, por fabor.

Follow me, please.

1 Warm up (1 minute)

What are "breakfast", "lunch", and "dinner" in Spanish? (pp.20-1)

Say "I", "you" (informal), "he", "she", "we", "you" (plural/formal), "they" (masculine), "they" (feminine). (pp.14-15)

QUERER
To want

Querer (*to want*) is a verb that is essential to everyday conversation. There is also a polite form, **quisiera** (*I'd like*). Use this when requesting something because quiero (*I want*) may sound too strong: **¿Qué quiere beber?** (*What do you want to drink?*); **Quisiera una cerveza** (*I'd like a beer*).

2 Querer: to want (6 minutes)

Say the different forms of **querer** (*to want*) aloud. Use the cover flap to test yourself and, when you are confident, practise the sample sentences below.

yo quiero *yoh kyairoh*	I want
tú quieres/usted quiere *too kyaires/oosted kyairay*	you want (singular, informal/formal)
él/ella quiere *el/eh-yah kyairay*	he/she wants
nosotros/-as queremos *nosotros/-as keraymos*	we want (masculine/feminine)
vosotros/-as queréis/ ustedes quieren *bosotros/-as kerays/ oostedes kyairen*	you want (plural, informal/formal)
ellos/-as quieren *eh-yos/-as-yas kyairen*	they want (masculine/feminine)
¿Quieres vino? *kyaires beenoh?*	Do you want some wine?
Quiere un coche nuevo. *kyairay oon kochay nweboh*	She wants a new car.

Quiero caramelos.
kyairoh karamelos
I want some sweets.

Conversational tip Although it may sound rude to you, Spaniards don't say *please* (**por favor**) or *thank you* (**gracias**) very often, and they hardly ever say *excuse me* (**perdón**) or *I'm sorry* (**lo siento**), but they use the tone of their voices and choice of words to imply politeness, such as **quisiera** (*I'd like*) instead of **quiero** (*I want*).

3 Polite requests (4 minutes)

Practise the following sample phrases that use **quisiera** (*I'd like*), the form of **quiero** (*I want*) that is used for polite requests.

I'd like a beer.	**Quisiera un cerveza.** *keesyairah oon therbaythah*

I'd like a table for tonight.	**Quisiera una mesa para esta noche.** *keesyairah oonah mesah parah estah nocheh*

I'd like to see the menu, please.	**Quisiera ver la carta, por favor.** *keesyairah ber lah kartah, por fabor*

4 Put into practice (4 minutes)

Join in this conversation. Read the Spanish beside the pictures on the left and follow the instructions to make your reply. Then test yourself by concealing the answers using the cover flap.

Buenas tardes señor. ¿Tiene una reserva?
bwenas tardes senyor. tyeneh oonah reserbah

No, pero quisiera una mesa para tres.
noh, peroh keesyairah oonah mesah parah tres

Good evening, sir. Do you have a reservation?

Say: No, but I would like a table for three.

Muy bien. ¿Qué mesa le gustaría?
mwee byen. kay mesah le goostareeyah

Cerca de la ventana, por favor.
therkah day lah bentanah, por fabor

Very good. Which table would you like?

Say: Near the window please.

1 Warm up (1 minute)

Say "She's happy" and
"I'm not sure". (pp.14-15)

Ask "Do you have
churros?" (pp.18-19)

Say "I'd like a white
coffee". (pp.18-19)

LOS PLATOS
Dishes

Spain offers a large variety of regional dishes. Plenty of
garlic and olive oil are a feature of many typical dishes.
Not many restaurants offer a vegetarian menu, but
there are, however, many traditional Spanish dishes
that do not contain meat. Ask your waiter for advice.

Cultural tip At lunch time, you will find that many
restaurants offer **el menú del día** (*the day's set menu*).
This is usually a three-course meal, with bread and
drink included in the price.

2 Match and repeat (4 minutes)

Match the numbered items to
the Spanish words in the panel.

1 las verduras
las berdooras

2 la fruta
lah frootah

3 el queso
el kesoh

4 los frutos secos
los frootos sekos

5 la sopa
lah sopah

6 las aves
las ahbes

7 el pescado
el peskadoh

8 la pasta
lah pastah

9 el marisco
el mareeskoh

10 la carne
lah karnay

fruit **2**

vegetables **1**

cheese **3**

5 soup

poultry **6**

8 pasta

9 seafood

3 Words to remember: cooking methods (3 minutes)

The ending often varies depending on the gender of item described.

fried (m/f)	**frito/-a**	_free_toh/-ah
grilled	**a la plancha**	ah lah _plan_chah
roasted (m/f)	**asado/-a**	ah_sa_doh/-ah
boiled (m/f)	**hervido/-a**	er_bee_doh/-ah
steamed	**al vapor**	al ba_por_
rare (m/f)	**poco hecho/-a**	pokoh _eh_-choh/-ah

Quisiera mi filete bien hecho.
_kee_syairah mee _feele_tay byen _eh_-choh
I'd like my steak well done.

6 Say it (2 minutes)

What is **tortilla**?

I'm allergic to seafood.

I'd like a beer.

nuts **4**

fish **7**

10 meat

4 Words to remember: drinks (3 minutes)

Familiarize yourself with these words.

water	**el agua**	el _ah_gwah
fizzy water	**el agua con gas**	el _ah_gwah kon gas
still water	**el agua sin gas**	el _ah_gwah seen gas
wine	**el vino**	el _bee_noh
beer	**la cerveza**	lah thair_bay_thah
fruit juice	**el zumo**	el _thoo_moh

5 Useful phrases (2 minutes)

Learn these phrases and then test yourself.

I am a vegetarian. (m/f)	**Soy vegetariano/-a.**	soy be-hetar_ee_anoh/-ah
I am allergic to nuts. (m/f)	**Soy alérgico/-a a los frutos secos.**	soy ah_ler_-heekoh/-ah ah los _froo_tos _se_kos
What is "conejo"?	**¿Qué es "conejo"?**	kay es ko_ne_-hoh

REPASE Y REPITA
Review and repeat

1 What food?

1 los frutos secos
los frootos sekos

2 el marisco
el mareeskoh

3 la carne
lah karnay

4 el azúcar
el ah-thookar

5 la copa
lah kopah

1 What food? (4 minutes)

Name the numbered items.

1 nuts

sugar **4**

seafood **2**

meat **3**

glass **5**

2 This is my...

1 Ésta es mi mujer.
estah es mee moo-hair

2 Aquí están sus hijas.
ahkee estan soos ee-has

3 Su mesa es de no fumadores.
soo mesah es day noh foomadores

2 This is my... (4 minutes)

Say these phrases in Spanish. Use **mi(-s)**, **tu(-us)** or **su(-s)**.

1 This is my wife.
2 Here are her daughters.
3 Their table is non-smoking.

3 I'd like...

1 Quisiera un café.
keesyairah oon kafay

2 Quisiera churros.
keesyairah choorros

3 Quisiera azúcar.
keesyairah ah-thookar

4 Quisiera un café con leche.
keesyairah oon kafay kon lechay

3 I'd like... (3 minutes)

Say "I'd like" the following:

1 black coffee　churros **2**　**3** sugar

white coffee **4**

6 pasta

knife 7

8 cheese

beer 10

9 napkin

1 What food?

6 la pasta
lah *pastah*

7 el cuchillo
el koo*chee*-yoh

8 el queso
el *kesoh*

9 la servilleta
lah serbee-*yetah*

10 la cerveza
lah thair*baythah*

4 Restaurant (4 minutes)

You arrive at a restaurant. Join in the conversation,
replying in Spanish following the English prompts.

Buenas tardes señora, señor.
1 Ask for a table for six.

¿Fumadores o no fumadores?
2 Say: non-smoking.

Síganme, por favor.
3 Ask for the menu.

¿Quiere la carta de vinos?
4 Say: No. Fizzy water, please.

Muy bien.
5 Say you don't have a glass.

4 Restaurant

**1 Buenas tardes,
quisiera una mesa
para seis.**
bwenas *tardes,
kee*syairah *oonah
mesah parah* seys

2 No fumadores.
noh foomadores

3 La carta, por favor.
lah *kartah*, por *fabor*

**4 No. Agua con gas,
por favor.**
noh. *ah*gwah kon gas,
por *fabor*

5 No tengo copa.
noh *tengoh kopah*

LOS DÍAS Y LOS MESES
Days and months

In Spanish, *days of the week* (**los días de la semana**) and *months* (**los meses**) do not have capital letters Notice that you use **en** with months: **en abril** (*in April*), but **el** or **los** with days: **el/los lunes** (*on Monday/Mondays*).

2 **Words to remember: days of the week** (5 minutes)

Familiarize yourself with these words and test yourself using the cover flap.

lunes *loones*	Monday
martes *martes*	Tuesday
miércoles *myairkoles*	Wednesday
jueves *hwebes*	Thursday
viernes *byernes*	Friday
sábado *sabadoh*	Saturday
domingo *domeengoh*	Sunday
hoy *oy*	today
mañana *manyanah*	tomorrow
ayer *ah-yair*	yesterday

Nos reunimos mañana.
mos reh-ooneemos manyanah
We meet tomorrow.

Tengo una reserva para hoy.
tengoh oonah reserbah parah oy
I have a reservation for today.

3 **Useful phrases: days** (2 minutes)

Learn these phrases and then test yourself using the cover flap.

La reunión no es el martes. *lah reh-oonyon noh es el martes*	The meeting isn't on Tuesday.
Trabajo los domingos. *traba-hoh los domeengos*	I work on Sundays.

4 Words to remember: months (5 minutes)

Familiarize yourself with these words and test yourself using the cover flap.

Nuestro aniversario es en julio.
nwestroh aneebairsaree-oh es en hoolee-oh
Our anniversary is in July.

Navidad es en diciembre.
nabeedad es en deethyembray
Christmas is in December.

January	**enero**	*ehneroh*
February	**febrero**	*febreroh*
March	**marzo**	*marthoh*
April	**abril**	*abreel*
May	**mayo**	*mah-yoh*
June	**junio**	*hoonee-oh*
July	**julio**	*hoolee-oh*
August	**agosto**	*agostoh*
September	**septiembre**	*septyembray*
October	**octubre**	*oktoobray*
November	**noviembre**	*nobyembray*
December	**diciembre**	*deethyembray*
month	**el mes**	*el mes*
year	**el año**	*el anyoh*

5 Useful phrases: months (2 minutes)

Learn these phrases and then test yourself using the cover flap.

My children are on holiday in August.	**Mis hijos están de vacaciones en agosto.** *mees ee-hos estan day bakathyones en agostoh*
My birthday is in June.	**Mi cumpleaños es en junio.** *mee koomplay-anyos es en hoonee-oh*

LA HORA Y LOS NÚMEROS
Time and numbers

1 Warm up (1 minute)

Count in Spanish from 1 to 10. (pp.10-11)

Say "I have a reservation". (pp.20-1)

Say "The meeting is on Wednesday". (pp.28-9)

The hour is preceded by **la** as in **la una** (*one o'clock*) and **las** for the other numbers: **las dos**, **las tres**, and so on. In English the minutes come first: ten to five, in Spanish the hour comes first: **las cinco menos diez** (*five minus ten*).

2 Words to remember: time (4 minutes)

Memorize how to tell the time in Spanish.

la una *lah oonah*	one o'clock
la una y cinco *lah oonah ee theenkoh*	five past one
la una y cuarto *lah oonah ee kwartoh*	quarter past one
la una y veinte *lah oonah ee beyntay*	twenty past one
la una y media *lah oonah ee medee-ah*	half past one
las dos menos cuarto *las dos menos kwartoh*	quarter to two
las dos menos diez *las dos menos dyeth*	ten to two

3 Useful phrases (2 minutes)

Learn these phrases and then test yourself using the cover flap.

¿Qué hora es? *kay orah es*	What time is it?
¿A qué hora quiere el desayuno? *ah kay orah kyairay el desah-yoonoh*	What time do you want breakfast?
La reunión es a mediodía. *lah reh-oonyon es ah maydyodee-ah*	The meeting is at midday.

4 Words to remember: higher numbers (6 minutes)

To say 21 you use **veinti** and add **uno** (*one*): **veintiuno**. Successive numbers are created in the same way – for example, **veintidós** (22), **veintitrés** (23), and so on. After 30 link the numbers with **y** (*and*): **treinta y uno** (31), **cuarenta y cinco** (45), **sesenta y seis** (66).

Note the special forms used for 500, 700, and 900: **quinientos**, **setecientos**, and **novecientos**.

Quiero el autobús cincuenta y tres.
kyairoh el aootoboos theenkwentah ee tres
I want the number 53 bus.

eleven	**once** *onthay*
twelve	**doce** *dothay*
thirteen	**trece** *trethay*
fourteen	**catorce** *katorthay*
fifteen	**quince** *keenthay*
sixteen	**dieciséis** *deeaytheeseyees*
seventeen	**diecisiete** *deeaytheesyeytay*
eighteen	**dieciocho** *deeaythyochoh*
nineteen	**diecinueve** *deeaythynwebay*
twenty	**veinte** *beyntay*
thirty	**treinta** *treyntah*
forty	**cuarenta** *kwarentah*
fifty	**cincuenta** *theenkwentah*
sixty	**sesenta** *sesentah*
seventy	**setenta** *setentah*
eighty	**ochenta** *ochentah*
ninety	**noventa** *nobentah*
hundred	**cien** *theeayn*
two hundred	**doscientos** *dos-theeayntos*
five hundred	**quinientos** *keeneeayntos*
thousand	**mil** *meel*
two thousand	**dos mil** *dos meel*
one million	**un millón** *oon mee-yon*

5 Say it (2 minutes)

25

68

84

91

five to ten

half past eleven

What time is lunch?

LAS CITAS
Appointments

1 **Warm up** (1 minute)

Say the days of the week.
(pp.28-9)

Say "three o'clock".
(pp.30-1)

What's the Spanish for
"today", "tomorrow", and
"yesterday"? (pp.28-9)

Business in Spain is generally conducted more
formally than in Britain or the United States. The
Spanish also tend to leave the office for the lunch
hour, often having a sit-down meal. Remember to
use the formal forms of *you* (**usted**, **ustedes**) in
business situations.

Bienvenido.
byenveneedoh
Welcome.

2 **Useful phrases** (5 minutes)

Learn these phrases and then test yourself.

¿Nos reunimos mañana? *nos reh-ooneemos manyanah*	Shall we meet tomorrow?
¿Con quién? *kon kee-en*	With whom?
¿Cuándo está libre? *kwandoh esta leebray*	When are you free?
Lo siento, estoy ocupado(-a). *loh syentoh, estoy okoopadoh(-ah)*	I'm sorry, I am busy.
¿Qué tal el jueves? *keh tal el hwebes*	How about Thursday?
A mí me va bien. *ah mee may bah byen*	That's good for me.

el apretón de manos
el apreton day manos
handshake

3 **In conversation** (4 minutes)

Buenos días. Tengo una cita.
bwenos deeyas. tengoh oonah theetah

Good morning. I have an appointment.

¿Con quién es la cita?
kon kee-en es lah theetah

With whom is the appointment?

Con el Señor Montoya.
kon el senyor montoyah

With Mr Montoya.

4 Put into practice (5 minutes)

Join in this conversation. Read the Spanish beside the pictures on the left and then follow the instructions to make your reply. Then test yourself by concealing the answers on the right with the cover flap.

¿Nos reunimos el jueves?
nos reh-oo<u>nee</u>mos el <u>hwe</u>bes?

Shall we meet Thursday?

Say: Sorry, I'm busy.

Lo siento, estoy ocupado(-a).
loh <u>syen</u>toh, estoy okoo<u>pa</u>doh(-ah)

¿Cuándo está libre?
<u>kwan</u>doh es<u>ta</u> <u>lee</u>bray

When are you free?

Say: Tuesday afternoon.

El martes por la tarde.
el <u>mar</u>tes por lah <u>tar</u>day

A mí me va bien.
ah mee may bah byen

That's good for me.

Ask: At what time?

¿A qué hora?
ah kay <u>o</u>rah

A las cuatro, si a usted le va bien.
ah las <u>kwa</u>troh, see ah oos<u>ted</u> le bah byen

At four o'clock, if that's good for you.

Say: Yes, it's good for me.

Sí, me va bien.
see, may bah byen

Muy bien. ¿A qué hora?
mwee byen. ah kay <u>o</u>rah?

Very good. What time?

A las tres, pero llego un poco tarde.
ah las tres, <u>pe</u>roh <u>ye</u>goh oon <u>po</u>koh <u>tar</u>day

At three o'clock, but I'm a little late.

No se preocupe. Tome asiento, por favor.
noh say pre-oh<u>koo</u>pay. <u>to</u>may asy<u>ain</u>toh, por <u>fa</u>bor

Don't worry. Take a seat, please.

POR TELÉFONO
On the telephone

1 **Warm up** (1 minute)

Say "I'm sorry". (pp.32-3)

What is the Spanish for "I'd like an appointment". (pp.32-3)

How do you say "when?" in Spanish? (pp.32-3)

The emergency number for police, ambulance, or fire services is 112. For directory enquiries dial 11818. Telephone cards can be used with public or private phones by tapping in a code. Available from newsagents and tobacconists, they are a cheap way to call overseas.

2 **Match and repeat** (4 minutes)

Match the numbered items to the Spanish in the panel on the left, then test yourself.

1 **el cargador**
el kargador

2 **el contestador automático**
el kontestador aootomateekoh

3 **la tarjeta telefónica**
lah tarhetah telefoneekah

4 **el móvil**
el mobeel

5 **los auriculares**
los aooreekoolares

charger **1**

headphones **5**

mobile **4**

phone card **3**

3 **In conversation** (4 minutes)

Dígame, Susana Castillo al habla.
deegamay, soosanah kasteeyoh al ablah

Hello. Susana Castillo speaking.

Buenos días. Quisiera hablar con Julián López, por favor.
bwenos deeyas. keesyair-ah ablar kon hooleean lopeth, por fabor

Hello. I'd like to speak to Julián López, please.

¿De parte de quién?
day partay day kee-en?

Who's speaking?

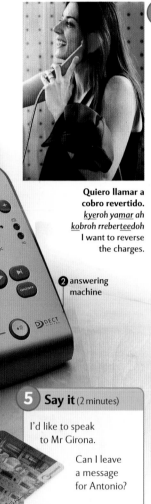

4 Useful phrases (4 minutes)

Practise these phrases and then test yourself using the cover flap.

Quisiera una línea externa.
keesyairah oonah leeneah externah

I'd like an outside line.

Quiero llamar a cobro revertido.
kyeroh yamar ah kobroh rreberteedoh
I want to reverse the charges.

❷ answering machine

Quisiera hablar con María Alfaro.
keesyairah ablar kon mareeah alfaroh

I'd like to speak to María Alfaro.

¿Puedo dejar un mensaje?
pwedoh dehar oon mensahay

Can I leave a message?

5 Say it (2 minutes)

I'd like to speak to Mr Girona.

Can I leave a message for Antonio?

Perdone, me he equivocado de número.
perdonay, may ay ekeebokadoh day noomeroh

Sorry, I have the wrong number.

José Ortega, de Imprentas Lacuesta.
hosay ortegah, day eemprentas lakwestah

José Ortega of Lacuesta Printers.

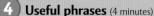

Lo siento. La línea está comunicando.
loh syaintoh. lah leeneah estah komooneekandoh

I'm sorry. The line is busy.

¿Le puede decir que me llame, por favor?
lay pweday detheer kay may yamay, por fabor

Can you ask him to call me, please?

REPASE Y REPITA
Review and repeat

Respuestas
Answers (Cover with flap)

1 Sums

❶ dieciséis
deeaytheesayees

❷ treinta y nueve
treyntah ee nwebay

❸ cincuenta y tres
theenkwentah ee tres

❹ setenta y cuatro
setentah ee kwatroh

❺ noventa y nueve
nobentah ee nwebay

1 Sums (4 minutes)

Say the answers to these sums out loud in Spanish. Then check you have remembered correctly.

❶ 10 + 6 = ?
❷ 14 + 25 = ?
❸ 66 - 13 = ?
❹ 40 + 34 = ?
❺ 90 + 9 = ?

3 Telephones (3 minutes)

What are the numbered items in Spanish?

❶ mobile

phone card ❸

2 I want...

❶ Quiere
kyairay

❷ quiere
kyairay

❸ queremos
keraymos

❹ quieres
kyaires

❺ quieren
kyairen

❻ quiero
kyairoh

2 I want... (3 minutes)

Fill the gaps with the correct form of (*to want*).

❶ ¿ _____ usted un café?

❷ Ella _____ ir de vacaciones.

❸ Nosotros _____ una mesa para tres.

❹ Tú _____ una cerveza.

❺ Ellos _____ una mesa para dos.

❻ Yo _____ caramelos.

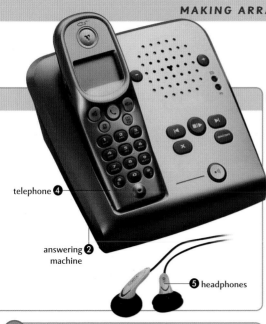

telephone ❹

answering ❷
machine

❺ headphones

Respuestas
Answers (Cover with flap)

3 Telephones

❶ **el móvil**
el mobeel

❷ **el contestador automático**
el kontestador aootomateekoh

❸ **la tarjeta telefónica**
lah tarhetah telefoneekah

❹ **el teléfono**
el telefonoh

❺ **los auriculares**
los aooreekoolares

4 When? (2 minutes)

What do these sentences mean?

❶ **Tengo una cita el lunes veinte de mayo.**

❷ **Mi cumpleaños es en septiembre.**

❸ **Hoy es domingo.**

❹ **No trabajo en agosto.**

4 When?

❶ I have a meeting on Monday, 20th May.

❷ My birthday is in September.

❸ Today is Sunday.

❹ I don't work in August.

5 Time (3 minutes)

Say these times in Spanish.

❶ ❷ ❸

❹ ❺ ❻

5 Time

❶ **la una**
lah oonah

❷ **la una y cinco**
la oonah ee theenkoh

❸ **la una y veinte**
lah oonah ee beyntay

❹ **la una y media**
lah oonah ee medee-ah

❺ **la una y cuarto**
lah oonah ee kwartoh

❻ **las dos menos diez**
las dos menos dyeth

1 Warm up (1 minute)

Count to 100 in tens.
(pp.10-11, pp.30-1)

Ask "What time is it?"
(pp.30-1)

Say "Half-past one".
(pp.30-1)

EN LA OFICINA DE BILLETES
At the ticket office

In Spain, commuter trains are very good value, clean, and efficient. Long-distance trains still offer smoking and non-smoking carriages, and the prices vary depending on what day you travel, blue days being the cheapest.

2 Words to remember (3 minutes)

Learn these words and then test yourself.

la estación *lah estathyon*	(train) station
la terminal *lah termeenal*	(bus) station
el billete *el beeyetay*	ticket
de ida *day eedah*	single
de ida y vuelta *day eedah ee bweltah*	return
de primera *day preemerah*	first class
de segunda *day segoondah*	second class
el descuento *el deskwentoh*	discount

el pasajero
el pasahairoh
passenger

la señal
lah senyal
sign

La estación está llena de gente.
lah estathyon estah yenah day hentay
The station is crowded.

3 In conversation (4 minutes)

Dos billetes para Bilbao, por favor.
dos beeyetes parah beeba-oh, por fabor

Two tickets for Bilbao, please.

¿De ida y vuelta?
day eedah y bweltah

Return?

Si.¿Necesito reservar asiento?
see. netheseetoh rreseerbar asyaintoh

Yes. Do I need to reserve seats?

4 Useful phrases (5 minutes)

Mi tren va con retraso.
mee tren bah kon rretrasoh
My train is late.

el tren	el andén
el tren	*el anden*
train	platform

Learn these phrases and then test yourself using the cover flap.

How much is a ticket to Madrid?	**¿Cuánto cuesta un billete para Madrid?** *kwantoh kwaystah oon beeyetay parah madreed*
Can I pay by credit card?	**¿Puedo pagar con tarjeta de crédito?** *pwedoh pagar kon tarhetah day kredeetoh*
Do I have to change?	**¿Tengo que cambiar?** *tengoh kay kambee-ar*
Which platform does the train leave from?	**¿De qué andén sale el tren?** *day kay anden salay el tren*
Are there any discounts?	**¿Hay algún descuento?** *ah-ee algoon deskwentoh*
What time does the train for Gijón leave?	**¿A qué hora sale el tren para Gijón?** *ah kay orah salay el tren parah geehon*

5 Say it (2 minutes)

Which platform does the train for Madrid leave from?

Three return tickets to Murcia, please.

Cultural tip Most train stations now have automatic ticket machines that also take credit cards.

No hace falta. Cuarenta euros, por favor.
noh ahthay faltah. kwarentah eh-ooros, por fabor

That's not necessary. Forty euros, please.

¿Aceptan tarjetas de crédito?
ahtheptan tarhetas day kredeetoh

Do you accept credit cards?

Si. El tren sale del andén cinco.
see. el tren salay del anden theenkoh

Yes. The train leaves from platform five.

1 Warm up (1 minute)

What is "train" in Spanish? (pp.38-9)

What does "¿De qué andén sale el tren?" mean? (pp.38-9)

Ask "When are you free?" (pp.32-3)

IR Y COGER
To go and to take

The verbs **ir** (to go) and **coger** (to take) allow you to create many useful sentences. Note that **coger** can also mean to catch: **coger una pelota** (to catch a ball), **coger un resfriado** (to catch a cold); to grab: **coger a alguien** (to grab someone); and to hold: **coger a un bebé** (to hold a baby).

2 Ir: to go (6 minutes)

Spanish uses the same form of **ir** for both I go and I am going: **voy a Madrid** (I am going to Madrid/I go to Madrid). The same is true of other verbs - for example, **cojo el metro** (I am taking the metro/I take the metro).

yo voy *yoh boy*	I go
tú vas/usted va *too bas/oos<u>ted</u> bah*	you go (informal/ formal singular)
él/ella va *el/<u>eh</u>-yah bah*	he/she goes
nosotros(-as) vamos *no<u>so</u>tros(-as) <u>b</u>amos*	we go
vosotros(-as) vais/ ustedes van *bo<u>so</u>tros(-as) baees/ oos<u>te</u>des ban*	you go (informal/ formal plural)
ellos/ellas van *<u>eh</u>-yos/<u>eh</u>-yas ban*	they go
¿A dónde vas? *ah <u>don</u>day bas*	Where are you going?
Voy a Madrid. *boy ah ma<u>dreed</u>*	I am going to Madrid.

Voy a la Plaza de España.
boy ah lah <u>plathah</u> day es<u>pany</u>ah
I am going to the Plaza de España.

Conversational tip You may have noticed that **de** (of) combines with **el** to produce **del** as in **Museo del Prado** (meaning literally *museum of the Prado*); **el menú del día** (*menu of the day*). In the same way, **a** (to) combines with **el** to produce **al**: **Voy al museo** (*I'm going to the museum*). With feminine and plural words **de** remains separate from **la**, **los**, and **las**.

3 Coger: to take (6 minutes)

Yo cojo el metro todos los días.
yoh kohoh el metroh todos los deeyas
I take the metro every day.

Say the present tense of **coger** (to take) aloud. Use the cover flap to test yourself. When you are confident, practise the sentences below.

yo cojo *yoh kohoh*	I take
tú coges/usted coge *too kohes/oosted kohay*	you take (informal/formal singular)
él/ella coge *el/eh-yah kohay*	he/she takes
nosotros(-as) cogemos *nosotros(-as) kohaymos*	we take
vosotros(-as) cogéis/ustedes cogen *bosotros(-as) kohe-ees/oostedes kohen*	you take (informal/formal plural)
ellos/ellas cogen *eh-yos/eh-yas kohen*	they take

No quiero coger un taxi. *noh kyairoh koher oon taksee*	I don't want to take a taxi.

Coja la primera a la izquierda. *kohah lah preemerah ah lah eethkyairdah*	Take the first on the left.

4 Put into practice (2 minutes)

Cover the text on the right and complete the dialogue in Spanish.

¿A dónde va?
ah donday bah

Where are you going?

Say: I'm going to the Puerta del Sol.

Voy a la Puerta del Sol.
boy ah lah pwertah del sol

¿Quiere coger el autobús?
kyairay koher el aootoboos

Do you want to take the bus?

Say: No, I want to go by metro.

No, quiero ir en metro.
noh, kyairoh eer en metroh

TAXI, AUTOBÚS, Y METRO
Taxi, bus, and metro

1 Warm up (1 minute)

Say "I don't want to take a taxi". (pp.40–41)

Ask "Where are you going?" (pp.40–41)

Say "80" and "40". (pp.30–31)

The metro and some buses operate a ticket system where you have to validate your tickets in a machine. There's a standard fare per ride, but you can also buy a **metrobús**, a book of 10 tickets for both buses and metro.

2 Words to remember (4 minutes)

Familiarize yourself with these words.

el autobús *el aootoboos*	bus/coach
la taquilla *lah takeeyah*	ticket office
la estación de metro *lah estathyon day metroh*	metro station
la parada de autobús *lah paradah day aootoboos*	bus stop
la tarifa *lah tareefah*	fare
el taxi *el taksee*	taxi
la parada de taxis *lah paradah day taksees*	taxi rank

¿Para aquí el 17?
parah ahkee el deeaytheeseeaytay
Does the number 17 bus stop here?

3 In conversation: taxi (2 minutes)

A la Plaza de España, por favor.
ah lah plathah day espanyah, por fabor

Plaza de España, please.

Sí, de acuerdo, señor.
see, day akwairdo, senyor

Yes, certainly, sir.

¿Me puede dejar aquí, por favor?
may pweday dehar ahkee, por fabor

Can you drop me here, please?

4 Useful phrases (4 minutes)

Practise these phrases and then test yourself using the cover flap.

I'd like a taxi to go to the Prado.	**Quisiera un taxi para ir al Prado.** *keesyairah oon taksee parah eer al prado*
When is the next bus?	**¿Cuándo sale el próximo autobús?** *kwandoh salay el prokseemoh aootoboos*
How do you get to the museum?	**¿Cómo se va al museo?** *komoh say bah al moosayoh*
How long is the journey?	**¿Cuánto dura el viaje?** *kwantoh doorah el beeahay*
Please wait for me.	**Espéreme, por favor.** *esperemay, por fabor*

Cultural tip Metro lines in Madrid are known by numbers and the names of the first and last stations. Look out for the relevant end station. The Madrid metro runs every day between 6.00am and 2.00am.

6 Say it (2 minutes)

Do you go near the train station?

Do you go near the Prado?

When is the next bus to Barcelona?

5 In conversation: bus (2 minutes)

¿Pasa cerca del museo?
pasah therkah del moosayoh

Do you go near the museum?

Sí. Son 80 céntimos.
see. son ochentah thenteemos

Yes. That's 80 cents.

Avíseme cuando lleguemos.
abeesemay kwandoh yeghemos

Tell me when we arrive.

EN LA CARRETERA
On the road

Warm up (1 minute)

How do you say "I have..."? (pp.14-15)

Say "my father", "my sister", and "my parents". (pp.10-11, pp.12-13)

Say "I'm going to Madrid". (pp.40-1)

Spanish **autopistas** (*motorways*) are fast but can be quite expensive. You will find signs for **el peaje** (*toll payment stations*). These have multiple lanes. Make sure you enter a green lane that allows payment by cash or credit card. Some lanes are for passholders or lorries only.

2 Match and repeat (4 minutes)

Match the numbered items to the list on the left, then test yourself.

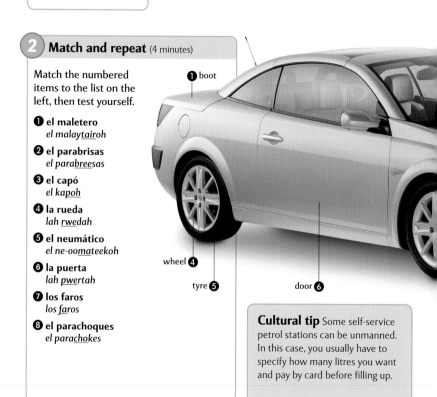

❶ boot

❶ **el maletero**
   el malaytairoh

❷ **el parabrisas**
   el parabreesas

❸ **el capó**
   el kapoh

❹ **la rueda**
   lah rwedah

❺ **el neumático**
   el ne-oomateekoh

❻ **la puerta**
   lah pwertah

❼ **los faros**
   los faros

❽ **el parachoques**
   el parachokes

wheel ❹

tyre ❺

door ❻

Cultural tip Some self-service petrol stations can be unmanned. In this case, you usually have to specify how many litres you want and pay by card before filling up.

3 Road features (2 minutes)

la rotonda
lah rrotonduh

roundabout

el semáforo
el semaforoh

traffic lights

el cruce
el kroothay

intersection

4 Useful phrases (4 minutes)

Learn these phrases and then test yourself using the cover flap.

The indicator doesn't work.	**El intermitente no funciona.** *el intairmeetaintay noh foonthyonah*
Fill it up, please.	**Lleno, por favor.** *yennoh, por fabor*

2 windscreen

3 bonnet

headlights **7**   **8** bumper

6 Say it (1 minute)

There's something wrong with my engine.

I have a flat tyre.

5 Match and repeat (3 minutes)

Familiarize yourself with these words then test yourself using the flap.

petrol	**la gasolina** *lah gasoleenah*
diesel	**el gasoil** *el gasoil*
oil	**el aceite** *el ah-thayeetay*
engine	**el motor** *el motor*
gearbox	**la caja de cambios** *lah kahah day kambyos*
indicator	**el intermitente** *el intairmeetaintay*
flat tyre	**la rueda pinchada** *lah rwaydah peenchadah*
exhaust	**el tubo de escape** *el tooboh day eskapay*
driving licence	**el carné de conducir** *el karnay day kondootheer*

la autopista
lah aootopeestah

motorway/expressway

la autopista de peaje
lah aootopeestah day pyahay

toll motorway

el atasco de tráfico
el ataskoh day trafeekoh

traffic jam

REPASE Y REPITA
Review and repeat

Respuestas
Answers (Cover with flap)

1 Transport

❶ el autobús
el aootoboos

❷ el taxi
el taksee

❸ el coche
el kochay

❹ la bicicleta
lah beetheekletah

❺ el metro
el metroh

1 Transport (3 minutes)

Name these forms of
transport in Spanish.

bus ❶

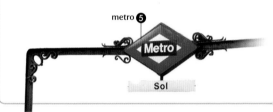

metro ❺

2 Go and take

❶ ir
eer

❷ cojo
kohoh

❸ va
bah

❹ vamos
bamos

❺ cogen
kohen

❻ voy
boy

2 Go and take (4 minutes)

Use the correct form of the verb in brackets.

❶ Quiero _____ a la estación. (ir)

❷ Yo _____ el metro. (coger)

❸ ¿A dónde _____ usted? (ir)

❹ Nosotros _____ al Museo del Prado. (ir)

❺ Ellos _____ un taxi. (coger)

❻ Yo _____ a Madrid. (ir)

③ car

② taxi

④ bicycle

③ You (4 minutes)

Use the correct form for **usted** or **tú** in each sentence.

❶ You are in a café. Ask "Do you have churros?"

❷ You are with a friend. Ask "Do you want a beer?"

❸ A visitor approaches you at your company reception. Ask "Do you have an appointment?"

❹ You are on the bus. Ask "Do you go near the station?"

❺ Ask your friend where she's going tomorrow.

Respuestas

Answers (Cover with flap)

③ You

❶ ¿Tiene churros?
tyenay choorros

❷ ¿Quieres una cerveza?
kyaires oonah thairbaythah

❸ ¿Tiene una cita?
tyenay oonah theetah

❹ ¿Pasa cerca de la estación?
pasah therkah day lah estathyon

❺ ¿A dónde vas mañana?
ah donday bas manyanah

④ Tickets (4 minutes)

You're buying tickets at a train station. Follow the conversation, replying in Spanish following the numbered English prompts.

¿Qué desea?
❶ I'd like two tickets to Sevilla.

¿De ida o de ida y vuelta?
❷ Return, please.

Muy bien. Cincuenta euros, por favor.
❸ What time does the train leave?

A las tres y diez.
❹ What platform does the train leave from?

Andén número siete.
❺ Thank you very much. Goodbye.

④ Tickets

❶ Quisiera dos billetes para Sevilla.
keesyairah dos beeyetes parah sebeeyah

❷ De ida y vuelta, por favor.
day eedah ee bweltah, por fabor

❸ ¿A qué hora sale el tren?
ah kay orah salay el tren

❹ ¿De qué andén sale el tren?
day kay anden salay el tren

❺ Muchas gracias. Adiós.
moochas grathyas. addy-os

EN LA CIUDAD
About town

1 Warm up (1 minute)

Ask "How do you get to the museum?" (pp.42-3)

Say "I want to take the metro" and "I don't want to take a taxi". (pp.40-1)

Note that the Spanish word **museo** (*museum*) also means art gallery when it's a public building in which works of art are exhibited; **galería de arte** usually refers to a shop that sells works of art. Be careful, too, not to confuse **librería** (*bookshop* or *bookshelf*) and **biblioteca** (*library*).

2 Match and repeat (4 minutes)

Match the numbered locations to the words in the panel.

❶ **el ayuntamiento**
   el ahyoonta-myaintoh

❷ **el puente**
   el pwentay

❸ **el centro**
   el thentroh

❹ **la iglesia**
   lah eegleseeah

❺ **la plaza**
   lah plathah

❻ **el aparcamiento**
   el aparka-myaintoh

❼ **la biblioteca**
   lah bibleeotekah

❽ **el museo**
   el moosayoh

❶ town hall   church ❹

city centre ❸

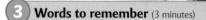

3 Words to remember (3 minutes)

Familiarize yourself with these words and test yourself using the cover flap.

la gasolinera *lah gasoleenerah*	petrol station
la oficina de información turística *lah ohfeetheenah day eenformathyon tooreesteekah*	tourist information
la piscina municipal *lah pistheenah mooneetheepal*	public swimming pool

❺ square

❼ library

Conversational tip In Spanish there are two ways of saying *am*, *is*, or *are*. You have already learned the verb **ser** (p.14): **soy inglés** (*I am English*); **es vegetariano** (*he is vegetarian*). When talking about where something is, you need to use a different verb: **estar**. The most important forms of this verb are: **estoy** (*I am*), **está** (*he/she/it is*), and **están** (*they are*): **¿Dónde están lla iglesia?** (*Where is the church?*); **El café no está lejos.** (*The café isn't far.*)

4 Useful phrases (4 minutes)

La catedral está en el centro.
lah katedral estah en el thentroh
The cathedral is in the city centre.

Practise these phrases and then test yourself using the cover flap.

Is there an art gallery in town?	**¿Hay algún museo de arte en la ciudad?** *ah-ee algoon moosayoh day artay en lah thyoodad*
Is it far from here?	**¿Está lejos de aquí?** *estah lehos day ahkee*
There is a swimming pool near the bridge.	**Hay una piscina cerca del puente.** *ah-ee oonah peestheenah therkah del pwentay*

5 Put into practice (3 minutes)

bridge ❷

car park ❻

museum ❽

Join in this conversation. Read the Spanish on the left and follow the instructions to make your reply. Then test yourself.

¿Le puedo ayudar? *lay pwedoh ahyoodar* Can I help you? Ask: Is there a library in town?	**¿Hay alguna biblioteca en la ciudad?** *ah-ee algoonah beebleeotekah en lah thyoodad*
No, pero hay un museo. *noh, peroh ah-ee oon moosayoh* No, but there's a museum. Ask: How do I get to the museum?	**¿Cómo se va al museo?** *komoh say bah al moosayoh*
Está por allí. *estah por ahyee* It's over there. Say: Thank you very much.	**Muchas gracias.** *moochas grathyas*

LAS DIRECCIONES
Directions

How do you say "near the station"? (pp.42-3)

Say "Take the first on the left". (pp.40-1)

Ask "Where are you going?" (pp.40-1)

You'll often be able to find a **plano de la ciudad** (*town map*) in the town centre, usually near the town hall or tourist office. In the older parts of Spanish towns there are often narrow streets, where you will usually find a one-way system in operation. Parking is usually restricted.

2 **Useful phrases** (4 minutes)

Learn these phrases and then test yourself.

Tuerza a la izquierda/ derecha. *twerthah ah lah eethkyairdah/derechah*	Turn left/right.
todo recto *todoh rrektoh*	straight on
¿Cómo se va a la piscina? *komoh say bah ah lah peestheenah*	How do I get to the swimming pool?
la primera a la derecha *lah preemerah ah lah derechah*	first right
la segunda a la izquierda *lah segoondah ah lah eethkyairdah*	second left

el bloque de oficinas
el blokay day ohfeetheenas
office block

la fuente
lah fwentay
fountain

3 **In conversation** (4 minutes)

¿Hay un restaurante en la ciudad?
ah-ee oon restaoorantay en la thyoodad

Is there a restaurant nearby?

Sí, cerca de la estación.
see, therkah day lah estathyon

Yes, near the station.

¿Cómo se va a la estación?
komoh say bah ah lah estathyon

How do I get to the station?

4 Words to remember (4 minutes)

Familiarize yourself with these words and test yourself using the flap.

traffic lights	**el semáforo** *el semaforoh*
corner	**la esquina** *lah eskeenah*
street/road	**la calle** *lah kayay*
main road	**la calle principal** *lah kayay preentheepal*
at the end of the street	**al final de la calle** *al feenal day lah kayay*
map	**el plano** *el planoh*
flyover	**el paso elevado** *el pasoh elebadoh*
opposite	**enfrente de** *enfrentay day*

Me he perdido.
may eh perdeedoh
I'm lost.

el centro deportivo
el thentroh deporteeboh
leisure centre

la zona peatonal
lah thonah pe-ahtonal
pedestrian zone

¿Dondé estamos?
donday estamos
Where are we?

5 Say it (2 minutes)

Turn right at the end of the street.

Turn left opposite the museum.

It's ten minutes by bus.

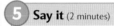

Tuerza a la izquierda en el semáforo.
twerthah ah lah eethkyairdah en el semaforoh

Turn left at the traffic lights.

¿Está lejos?
estah lehos

Is it far?

No, cinco minutos andando.
noh, theenkoh meenootos andandoh

No, it's five minutes on foot.

EL TURISMO
Sightseeing

1 **Warm up** (1 minute)

Say the days of the week in Spanish. (pp.28-9)

How do you say "six o'clock"? (pp.30-1)

Ask "What time is it?" (pp.30-1)

Most national museums and art galleries close on Mondays and public holidays. Although shops are normally closed on Sundays, many will open in tourist areas. In provincial areas, it is not unusual for public buildings and shops to close at lunchtime, between 1.30 and 4.30pm.

2 **Words to remember** (4 minutes)

Familiarize yourself with these words and test yourself using the flap.

la guía *lah gheeah*	guidebook
la entrada *lah entradah*	entrance ticket
el horario de apertura *el oraryoh day apertoorah*	opening times
el día festivo *el deeyah festeevoh*	public holiday
entrada libre *entradah leebray*	free entrance

la visita con guía
lah beeseetah kon gheeah
guided tour

Cultural tip If a public holiday falls on a Thursday or a Tuesday, people will often **hacer puente** (do a bridge) - in other words, they take Friday or Monday off as well, to make a long weekend.

3 **In conversation** (3 minutes)

¿Abren esta tarde?
ahbren estah tarday

Do you open
this afternoon?

Sí, pero cerramos a las cuatro.
see, peroh therramos ah las kwatroh

Yes, but we close at
four o'clock.

¿Tienen acceso para sillas de ruedas?
tyenen akthesoh parah seeyas day rwedas

Do you have access
for wheelchairs?

4 Useful phrases (3 minutes)

Practise these phrases and then test yourself using the cover flap.

What time do you open/close?	**¿A qué hora abre/cierra?** *ah kay orah ahbray/ thyairrah*
Where are the toilets?	**¿Dónde están los servicios?** *donday estan los serbeethyos*
Is there access for wheelchairs?	**¿Hay acceso para sillas de ruedas?** *ah-ee akthesoh parah seeyas day rwedas*

5 Put into practice (4 minutes)

Cover the text on the right and complete the dialogue in Spanish.

Lo siento, el museo está cerrado.
loh syentoh, el moosayoh estah therradoh

Sorry. The museum is closed.

Ask: Do you open on Tuesdays?

¿Abren los martes?
ahbren los martes

Sí, pero cerramos temprano.
see, peroh therramos tempranoh

Yes, but we close early.

Ask: At what time?

¿A qué hora?
ah kay orah

Sí, el ascensor está allí.
see, el asthensor estah ah-yee

Yes, there's a lift over there.

Gracias, quisiera cuatro entradas.
grathyas, keesyairah kwatroh entradas

Thank you, I'd like four entrance tickets.

Aquí tiene, y la guía es gratis.
ahkee tyenay, ee lah gheeah es gratees

Here you are, and the guidebook is free.

1 Warm up (1 minute)

Say "half past one".
(pp.30-1)

What's the Spanish for
"ticket"? (pp.38-9)

Say "I am going to New
York". (pp.40-1)

EN EL AEROPUERTO
At the airport

Although the airport environment is largely
international, it is sometimes useful to be able to
ask your way around the terminal in Spanish. It's a
good idea to make sure you have a few coins when
you arrive at the airport; you may need to pay for
a luggage trolley.

2 Words to remember (4 minutes)

Familiarize yourself with these words and
test yourself using the flap.

la facturación *lah faktoorathyon*	check-in
las salidas *las saleedas*	departures
las llegadas *las yehgadas*	arrivals
la aduana *lah adwanah*	customs
el control de pasaportes *el kontrol day pasaportes*	passport control
la terminal *lah termeenal*	terminal
la puerta de embarque *lah pwertah day embarkay*	boarding gate

**¿Cuál es la puerta de embarque
para el vuelo veintitrés?**
*kwal es lah pwertah day embarkay
parah el bweloh bayeenteetres*
Which is the boarding gate
for flight 23?

3 Useful phrases (3 minutes)

Learn these phrases and then test yourself
using the cover flap.

¿Sale a su hora el vuelo para Sevilla? *salay ah soo orah el bweloh parah seveeyah*	Is the flight for Seville on time?
No encuentro mi equipaje. *noh enkwentroh mee ehkeepahay*	I can't find my luggage.

4 Put into practice (3 minutes)

Join in this conversation. Read the Spanish on the left and follow the instructions to make your reply. Then test yourself by concealing the answers using the cover flap.

Hola, ¿le puedo ayudar?
o-lah, lay pwedoh ahyoodar

Hello, can I help you?

Ask: Is the flight to Madrid on time?

¿Sale a su hora el vuelo para Madrid?
salay ah soo orah el bweloh parah madreed

Sí señor.
see senyor

Yes sir.

Ask: Which is the boarding gate?

¿Cuál es la puerta de embarque?
kwal es lah pwertah day embarkay

5 Match and repeat (4 minutes)

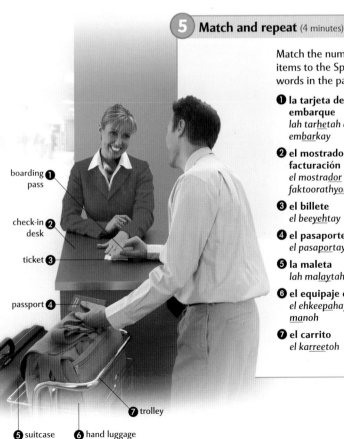

boarding pass ❶

check-in desk ❷

ticket ❸

passport ❹

❼ trolley

❺ suitcase   ❻ hand luggage

Match the numbered items to the Spanish words in the panel.

❶ **la tarjeta de embarque**
lah tarhetah day embarkay

❷ **el mostrador de facturación**
el mostrador day faktoorathyon

❸ **el billete**
el beeyehtay

❹ **el pasaporte**
el pasaportay

❺ **la maleta**
lah malaytah

❻ **el equipaje de mano**
el ehkeepahay day manoh

❼ **el carrito**
el karreetoh

Respuestas
Answers (Cover with flap)

REPASE Y REPITA
Review and repeat

1 Places

1 el museo
el moosayoh

2 el ayuntamiento
el ahyoonta-myaintoh

3 el puente
el pwentay

4 la biblioteca
lah beeblee-ohtekah

5 el aparcamiento
el ahparka-myaintoh

6 la catedral
lah katedral

7 la plaza
lah plathah

1 Places (4 minutes)

Name the numbered places in Spanish.

1 museum

2 town hall

3 bridge

4 library

5 car park

6 cathedral

square **7**

2 Car parts

1 el parabrisas
el parabreesas

2 el intermitente
el intairmee-taintay

3 el capó
el kapoh

4 el neumático
el ne-oomateekoh

5 la puerta
lah pwertah

6 el parachoques
el parachokes

2 Car parts (3 minutes)

Name these car parts in Spanish.

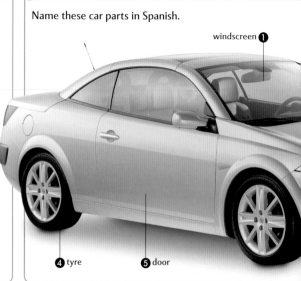
windscreen **1**

4 tyre

5 door

3 **Questions** (4 minutes)

Ask the questions that match these answers.

❶ El autobús sale a las ocho.
el aootoboos salay ah las ochoh

❷ El café es un euro cincuenta.
el kafay es oon eh-ooro theenkwentah

❸ No, no quiero vino.
noh, noh kyairoh beenoh

❹ El tren sale del andén cinco.
el tren salay del anden theenkoh

❺ Nosotros vamos a León.
nosotros bamos ah leh-on

❻ El próximo tren es dentro
de quince minutos.
*el prokseemoh tren es dentroh
day keenthay meenootos*

3 **Questions**

❶ ¿A qué hora sale
el autobús?
*ah kay orah salay
el aootoboos*

❷ ¿Cuánto es el café?
kwantoh es el kafay

❸ ¿Quieres vino?
kyaires beenoh

❹ ¿De qué andén sale
el tren?
*day kay anden salay
el tren*

❺ ¿A dónde vais?
ah donday baees

❻ ¿Cuándo es el
próximo tren?
*kwandoh es el
prokseemoh tren*

❷ indicator

❸ bonnet

❻ bumper

4 **Verbs** (4 minutes)

Choose the correct
form of the verb in
brackets to fill the gaps.

❶ Yo _____ inglés. (ser)

❷ Nosotros _____ el
metro. (tomar)

❸ Ella _____ a Marbella.
(ir)

❹ Él _____ casado.
(estar)

❺ ¿Tú _____ un té?
(querer)

❻ ¿Cuántos niños _____
usted? (tener)

4 **Verbs**

❶ soy
soy

❷ cogemos
kohaymos

❸ va
bah

❹ está
estah

❺ quieres
kyaires

❻ tiene
tyenay

1 **Warm up** (1 minute)

Ask "Do you accept credit cards?" (pp.38-9)

Ask "How much is that?" (pp.18-19)

Ask "Do you have children?" (pp.10-11)

RESERVAR UNA HABITACIÓN
Booking a room

Types of accommodation in Spain include: **hotel**, categorized from one to five stars; **pensión**, a small family-run hotel; **hostal**, cheap and basic; and **parador**, state-owned hotels in historic properties or places of great beauty.

2 **Useful phrases** (3 minutes)

Practise these phrases and then test yourself by concealing the Spanish on the left using the cover flap.

¿El desayuno está incluido?
el desayoonoh estah inklooeedoh

Is breakfast included?

¿Aceptan animales de compañía?
atheptan aneemales day kompanyeeah

Do you accept pets?

¿Tienen servicio de habitaciones?
tyenen serbeethyoh day abeetathyones

Do you have room service?

¿A qué hora tengo que dejar la habitación?
ah kay orah tengoh kay dehar lah abeetathyon

What time do I have to leave the room?

3 **In conversation** (5 minutes)

¿Tiene habitaciones libres?
tyenay abeetathyones leebres

Do you have any vacancies?

Sí, una habitación doble.
see, oonah abeetathyon doblay

Yes, a double room.

¿Tiene una cuna?
tyenay oonah koonah

Do you have a cot?

4 **Words to remember** (4 minutes)

Familiarize yourself with these words and test yourself by concealing the Spanish on the right using the cover flap.

¿Tiene la habitación vistas al parque?
tyenay lah abeetathyon beestas al parkay
Does the room have a view over the park?

room	**la habitación** *lah abeetathyon*
single room	**la habitación individual** *lah abeetathyon indeebeedwal*
double room	**la habitación doble** *lah abeetathyon doblay*
bathroom	**el cuarto de baño** *el kwartoh day banyoh*
shower	**la ducha** *lah doochah*
breakfast	**el desayuno** *el desayoonoh*
key	**la llave** *lah yabay*
balcony	**el balcón** *el balkon*
air-conditioning	**el aire acondicionado** *el ah-eeray akondeethyonadoh*

5 **Say it** (2 minutes)

Do you have a single room, please?

For six nights.

Is breakfast included?

Cultural tip Large hotels and **paradors** are generally the only types of hotel to offer breakfast, but you will generally be charged extra for it. If your accommodation doesn't provide breakfast, you'll usually find it easy to discover a bar or a café nearby where you can go for **café con leche** in the mornings.

Sí, claro. ¿Cuántas noches?
see, klaroh. kwantas noches

Yes, of course. How many nights?

Para tres noches.
parah tres noches

For three nights.

Muy bien. Aquí tiene la llave.
mwee byen. ahkee tyenay lah yabay

Very good. Here's the key.

EN EL HOTEL
In the hotel

1 Warm up (1 minute)

Say "Is there...?" and "There isn't...". (pp.48-9)

What does "¿Le puedo ayudar?" mean? (pp.54-5)

Although the larger hotels almost always have en-suite bathrooms, there are still some **pensiones** and **hostales** where you will have to share bathroom facilities and which usually don't provide towels. It is always advisable to check what is provided when you book.

2 Match and repeat (6 minutes)

Match the numbered items in this hotel bedroom with the Spanish text in the panel and test yourself using the cover flap.

❶ **la mesilla de noche**
   lah me<u>see</u>yah day nochay

❷ **la lámpara**
   lah <u>lam</u>parah

❸ **el equipo de música**
   el e<u>kee</u>poh day <u>moo</u>seekah

❹ **las cortinas**
   las kor<u>tee</u>nas

❺ **el sofá**
   el so<u>fah</u>

❻ **la almohada**
   lah almoh-<u>ah</u>dah

❼ **el cojín**
   el ko<u>heen</u>

❽ **la cama**
   lah <u>ka</u>mah

❾ **la colcha**
   lah <u>kol</u>chah

❿ **la manta**
   lah <u>man</u>tah

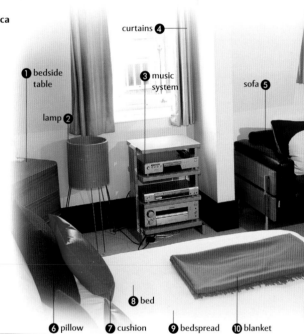

curtains ❹

❶ bedside table

❸ music system

sofa ❺

lamp ❷

❽ bed

❻ pillow   ❼ cushion   ❾ bedspread   ❿ blanket

Cultural tip When you arrive in your double room, you will usually see one long pillow instead of two individual ones on the bed. This is the usual pillow for a double bed - **cama de matrimonio** (literally, *marriage bed*). If you don't want to share your bed or pillow, you'll have to ask for **una habitación doble con dos camas** (*a double room with two beds*) to get a twin room.

3 Useful phrases (5 minutes)

Practise these phrases and then test yourself using the cover flap.

The room is too cold/hot.	**Hace demasiado frío/ calor en la habitación.** *ahthay daymasyahdoh freeoh/kalor en lah abeetathyon*

There are no towels.	**No hay toallas.** *noh ah-ee toh-ahyas*

I need some soap.	**Necesito jabón.** *netheseetoh habon*

The shower doesn't work.	**La ducha no funciona.** *lah doochah noh foonthyonah*

The lift is broken.	**El ascensor está roto.** *el asthensor estah rrotoh*

4 Put into practice (3 minutes)

Practise these phrases and then complete the dialogue in Spanish.

¿Le atienden? *lay atyainden*	**Necesito almohadas.** *netheseetoh almoh-ahdas*

Can I help you?

Say: I need some pillows.

La camarera se las llevará. *lah kamarairah say las yebarah*	**Y la televisión no funciona.** *ee lah telebeesyon noh foonthyonah*

The maid will bring some.

Say: And the TV doesn't work.

EN EL CÁMPING
At the campsite

Warm up (1 minute)

How do you ask
"Can I?" (pp.34-5)

Say "The lift is broken".
(pp.60-1)

Say "I need some towels".
(pp.60-1)

Camping is very popular in Spain. The country's
numerous campsites are well organized and operate
on a star system. The local tourist information office
will be able to offer a list of campsites in the area
together with their ratings. It is advisable to book
in advance during the summer months.

Useful phrases (3 minutes)

Learn these phrases and then test
yourself by concealing the Spanish
with the cover flap.

¿Puedo alquilar una bicicleta? _pwedoh alkeelar oonah beetheekletah_	Can I rent a bicycle?
¿Es el agua potable? _es el ahgwah potablay_	Is this drinking water?
¿Se permiten hogueras? _say permeeten ohgheras_	Are campfires allowed?
Las radios están prohibidas. _las rradyos estan proheebeedas_	Radios are forbidden.

¿Dónde está el grifo?
donday estah el greefoh
Where is the tap?

la oficina
lah ofeetheenah
office

el contenedor de la basura
el kontenedor day lah basoorah
litter bin

el doble techo
el doblay taychoh
fly sheet

In conversation (5 minutes)

Necesito una plaza para tres noches.
netheseetoh oonah plathah parah tres noches

I need a pitch for
three nights.

Hay una cerca de la piscina.
ah-ee oonah therkah day lah peestheenah

There's one near the
swimming pool.

¿Cuánto cuesta para una roulotte?
kwantoh kwestah parah oonah rroolot

How much is it for
a caravan?

5 Say it (2 minutes)

I need a pitch for four nights.

Can I rent a tent?

Where's the electrical hook-up?

los aseos
los asayos
toilets

el punto de luz
*el poontoh
day looth*
electrical hook-up

la cuerda
lah kwerdah
guy rope

la clavija
la klabeehah
tent peg

4 Words to remember (4 minutes)

Learn these words and then test yourself using the cover flap.

campsite	**el cámping** *el kampeen*
tent	**la tienda** *lah tyendah*
caravan	**la roulotte** *lah rroolot*
camper van	**la autocaravana** *la ah-ootokarabanah*
pitch	**la plaza** *lah plathah*
campfire	**la hoguera** *lah ohgherah*
drinking water	**el agua potable** *el ahgwah potablay*
rubbish	**la basura** *lah basoorah*
camping gas	**el camping-gas** *el kampeen gas*
showers	**las duchas** *las doochas*
sleeping bag	**el saco de dormir** *el sakoh day dormeer*
air mattress	**la colchoneta** *lah kolchonetah*
ground sheet	**el suelo aislante** *el sweloh ah-eeslantay*

Cincuenta euros. Una noche por adelantado.
theenkwentah eh-ooros. oonah nochay por adelantadoh

Fifty euros. One night in advance.

¿Puedo alquilar una barbacoa?
pwedoh alkeelar oonah barbakoh-ah

Can I rent a barbecue?

Sí, pero tiene que dejar una señal.
see, peroh tyenay kay dehar oonah senyal

Yes, but you must pay a deposit.

1 Warm up (1 minute)

How do you say "hot" and "cold"? (pp.60-1)

What is the Spanish for "room", "bed", and "pillow"? (pp.60-1)

DESCRIPCIONES
Descriptions

Adjectives are words used to describe things. In Spanish you generally put the adjective after the thing it describes in the same gender and number: **una bebida fría** (*a cold drink*, feminine singular); **un café frío** (*a cold coffee*, masculine singular); **dos bebidas frías** (*two cold drinks*, feminine plural).

2 Words to remember (7 minutes)

Adjectives change depending on whether the thing described is masculine (**el**) or feminine (**la**). Generally, a final **o** changes to **a** in the feminine, but if the adjective ends with **e** (such as **grande**) it doesn't change for the feminine. To form the plural, just add an **s**.

duro/dura *dooroh/doorah*	hard
blando/blanda *blandoh/blandah*	soft
caliente *kalyaintay*	hot
frío/fría *freeoh/freeah*	cold
grande *granday*	big
pequeño/pequeña *pekenyoh/pekenyah*	small
bonito/bonita *boneetoh/boneetah*	beautiful
feo/fea *feh-oh/feh-ah*	ugly
ruidoso/ruidosa *rrweedosoh/rrweedosah*	noisy
tranquilo/tranquila *trankeeloh/trankeelah*	quiet
bueno/buena *bwenoh/bwenah*	good
malo/mala *maloh/malah*	bad
lento/lenta *lentoh/lentah*	slow
rápido/rápida *rrapeedoh/rrapeedah*	fast

las montañas altas
las montanyas altas
high mountains

la tienda pequeña
lah tyaindah pekenyah
small shop

el coche viejo
el koche bee-ayhoh
old car

El pueblo es muy bonito.
el pwebloh es mwee boneetoh
The village is very beautiful.

la calle tranquila
lah kayay trankeelah
quiet road

3 Useful phrases (4 minutes)

Learn these phrases. Note that you can emphasize a description by using **muy** (*very*), **demasiado** (*too*), or **más** (*more*) before the adjective.

This coffee is cold.	**Este café está frío.** *estay kafay estah free-oh*
My room is very noisy.	**Mi habitación es muy ruidosa.** *mee abeetathyon es mwee rrweedosah*
My car is too small.	**Mi coche es demasiado pequeño.** *mee koche es demasyahdoh pekenyoh*
I need a softer bed.	**Necesito una cama más blanda.** *netheseetoh oonah kamah mas blandah*

4 Put into practice (3 minutes)

Join in this conversation. Cover up the text on the right and complete the dialogue in Spanish. Check and repeat if necessary.

Ésta es la habitación. *estah es lah abeetathyon* This is the bedroom. Say: The view is very beautiful.	**La vista es muy bonita.** *lah beestah es mwee boneetah*
El cuarto de baño está por ahí. *el kwartoh day banyoh estah por ah-ee* The bathroom is over there. Say: It is too small.	**Es demasiado pequeño.** *es demasyahdoh pekenyoh*
No tenemos otra. *noh tenaymos otrah* We haven't another. Say: It doesn't matter. We'll take the room.	**No importa. Nos quedamos con la habitación.** *noh importah. nos kedamos kon lah abeetathyon*

REPASE Y REPITA
Review and repeat

1 Descriptions

1 caliente
kalyaintay

2 pequeña
pekenyah

3 frío
free-oh

4 grande
granday

5 tranquila
trankeelah

1 Descriptions (3 minutes)

Put the word in brackets into Spanish. Use the correct masculine or feminine form.

1 El agua está demasiado _____. (hot)

2 La cama es muy _____. (small)

3 El café está _____. (cold)

4 Este cuarto de baño es más _____. (big)

5 Quisiera una habitación más _____. (quiet)

2 Campsite

1 el punto de luz
el poontoh day looth

2 la tienda
lah tyaindah

3 el contenedor de
la basura
*el kontenedor day
lah basoorah*

4 la cuerda
lah kwerdah

5 los aseos
los asayos

6 la roulotte
lah rroolot

2 Campsite (3 minutes)

Name these items you might find in a campsite.

tent **2**

guy rope **4**

electrical **1**
hook-up

litter bin **3**

3 At the hotel (4 minutes)

You are booking a room in a hotel. Follow the conversation, replying in Spanish where you can see the English prompts.

¿Qué desean?
❶ Do you have any vacancies?

Sí, una habitación doble.
❷ Do you accept pets?

Sí. ¿Cuántas noches?
❸ Three nights.

Son ciento cuarenta euros.
❹ Is breakfast included?

Sí. Aquí tiene la llave.
❺ Thank you very much.

3 At the hotel

❶ ¿Tiene habitaciones libres?
tyenay abeeta-thyones leebres

❷ ¿Aceptan animales de compañía?
atheptan aneemales day kompanyeeah

❸ Tres noches.
tres noches

❹ ¿El desayuno está incluido?
el desayoonoh estah inklooeedoh

❺ Muchas gracias.
moochas grathyas

4 Negatives (5 minutes)

Make these sentences negative using the verb in brackets.

❶ Yo _____ hijos. (tener)

❷ Ellos _____ a Madrid mañana. (ir)

❸ Él _____ un café. (querer)

❹ Yo _____ el metro. (coger)

❺ La vista _____ muy bonita. (ser)

4 Negatives

❶ no tengo
noh tengoh

❷ no van
noh ban

❸ no quiere
noh kyairay

❹ no cojo
noh kohoh

❺ no es
no es

❺ toilets

❻ caravan

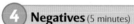

1 Warm up (1 minute)

Ask "How do I get to the station?" (pp.50-1)

Say "Turn left at the traffic lights" and "The station is opposite the café". (pp.50-1)

DE COMPRAS
Shopping

Small, traditional shops are still very common in Spain. But you can also find big supermarkets and shopping centres on the outskirts of cities. Local markets selling fresh, local produce can be found everywhere. Find out the market day from the **oficina de información turística** (*tourist office*).

2 Match and repeat (5 minutes)

Match the shops numbered 1 to 9 below and right to the Spanish in the panel. Then test yourself using the cover flap.

1 la panadería
lah panadaireeah

2 la pastelería
lah pastaylaireeah

3 el estanco
el estankoh

4 la carnicería
lah karnee-thaireeah

5 la charcutería
lah charkoo-taireeah

6 la librería
lah leebraireeah

7 la pescadería
lah peskadaireeah

8 la joyería
la hoyereeah

9 el banco
el bankoh

1 baker

2 cake shop

4 butcher

5 delicatessen

7 fishmonger

8 jeweller

Conversational tip If you want an everyday bar of soap or a tube of toothpaste, you need to go to a **droguería** (*drugstore*) rather than the **farmacia** (*pharmacy*). The **estanco** (*tobacconist*) is the place for all sorts of tobacco products and stamps. **Papelerías** cater for all your stationery needs. Most Spanish shops offer a free gift-wrapping service; you only need to ask: "**¿Me lo envuelve para regalo?**" (*May I have it gift-wrapped?*).

¿Dónde está la floristería?
donday estah lah floreestaireeah
Where is the florist?

❸ tobacconist

❻ bookshop

❾ bank

5 Say it (2 minutes)

Where is the bank?

Do you sell cheese?

Where do I pay?

3 Words to remember (4 minutes)

Familiarize yourself with these words and test yourself using the cover flap.

hardware shop	**la ferretería**	*lah ferretaireeah*
antique shop	**el anticuario**	*el anteekwareeoh*
hairdresser	**la peluquería**	*lah pelookaireeah*
greengrocer	**la verdulería**	*lah berdoolaireeah*
post office	**la oficina de correos**	*lah ofeetheenah day korrayos*
shoe shop	**la zapatería**	*lah thapataireeah*
dry cleaner	**la tintorería**	*lah teentoraireeah*
grocer	**el ultramarinos**	*el ooltramareenos*

4 Useful phrases (3 minutes)

Familiarize yourself with these phrases.

Where is the hairdresser?	**¿Dónde está la peluquería?**	*donday estah lah pelookaireeah*
Where do I pay?	**¿Dónde se paga?**	*donday say pagah*
I'm just looking, thank you.	**Sólo estoy mirando, gracias.**	*soloh estoy meerandoh grathyas*
Do you sell phonecards?	**¿Tiene tarjetas telefónicas?**	*tyenay tarhetas telefoneekas*
May I have two of those?	**¿Me pone dos de éstos?**	*may ponay dos day estos*
Can I place an order?	**¿Puedo hacer un pedido?**	*pwedoh ahther oon pedeedoh*

EN EL MERCADO
At the market

① Warm up (1 minute)

What is Spanish for "40", "56", "77", "82", and "94"? (pp.10-11 and pp.30-1)

Say "I'd like a big room". (pp.64-5)

Ask "Do you have a small car?" (pp.64-5)

Spain uses the metric system of weights and measures. You need to ask for the produce in kilogrammes or grammes. Some larger items, such as melons or pineapples, tend to be sold as **la pieza** (as single items); other items, such as lettuce, may be sold in lots of two or three.

② Match and repeat (4 minutes)

Match the numbered items in this scene with the text in the panel.

❶ los tomates
los to*mates*

❷ las judías
las hoo*dee*as

❸ los champiñones
los champee*nyo*nes

❹ las uvas
las *oo*bas

❺ los pepinos
los pe*pee*nos

❻ las alcachofas
las alka*cho*fas

❼ los guisantes
los *ghee*santes

❽ los pimientos
los pee*myain*tos

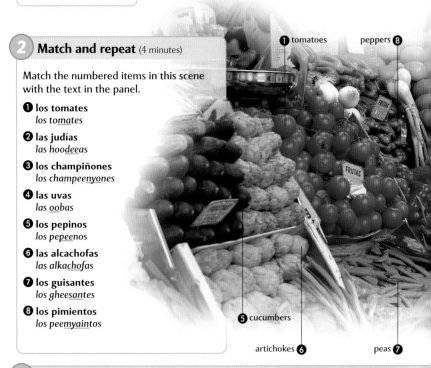

❶ tomatoes   peppers ❽

❺ cucumbers

artichokes ❻   peas ❼

③ In conversation: (3 minutes)

Quisiera tomates.
kee*syair*ah to*mates*

I'd like some tomatoes.

¿De los grandes o de los pequeños?
day los *gran*des oh day los pe*ken*yos

The large ones or the small ones?

Dos kilos de los pequeños, por favor.
dos *kee*los day los pe*ken*yos, por *fabor*

Two kilos of the small ones, please.

Cultural tip Spain uses the common European currency, the euro, which is divided into 100 **centimos**. Spanish-speaking countries in Central and South America all have their own currencies. Argentina, Chile, Uruguay, Colombia, and México all call their currency the **peso**, which is divided into 100 **centavos**.

grapes **4**
mushrooms **3**
beans **2**

4 Useful phrases (5 minutes)

Practise these phrases and then test yourself using the cover flap.

Esa salchicha es demasiado cara.
ehsah salcheechah es demasyahdoh karah

That sausage is too expensive.

¿A cuánto está esa?
ah kwantoh estah ehsa

How much is that one?

Eso es todo.
ehsoh es todoh

That'll be all.

5 Say it (2 minutes)

Two kilos of peas, please.

The mushrooms are too expensive.

How much are the grapes?

¿Algo más, señorita?
algoh mas, senyoreetah

Anything else, miss?

Eso es todo, gracias. ¿Cuánto es?
ehsoh es todoh, grathyas. kwantoh es

That'll be all, thank you. How much?

Tres cincuenta.
tres theenkwentah

Three fifty.

1 Warm up (1 minute)

What are these items you could buy in a supermarket? (pp.24–5)

la carne
el pescado
el queso
el zumo
el vino
el agua

EN EL SUPERMERCADO
At the supermarket

Prices in supermarkets are usually lower than in smaller shops. They offer all kinds of products, with the larger out-of-town **hipermercados** offering clothes, household goods, garden furniture, and DIY products.

2 Match and repeat (5 minutes)

Look at the numbered product categories and match them to the Spanish words in the panel on the left.

❶ **los productos del hogar**
los pro<u>dook</u>tos del oh<u>gar</u>

❷ **la fruta**
lah <u>froo</u>tah

❸ **las bebidas**
las be<u>bee</u>das

❹ **los platos preparados**
los <u>pla</u>tos prepa<u>ra</u>dos

❺ **los productos de belleza**
los pro<u>dook</u>tos day be<u>ye</u>thah

❻ **los productos lácteos**
los pro<u>dook</u>tos <u>lak</u>teh-os

❼ **la verdura**
lah ber<u>doo</u>rah

❽ **los congelados**
los konhe<u>la</u>dos

household ❶ products

fruit ❷

drinks ❸

ready meals ❹

vegetables ❼

frozen foods ❽

Cultural tip You cannot usually take unweighed fruit and vegetables sold by the kilo straight to the check-out at a supermarket. There is usually a separate counter or a self-service weighing machine.

3 Useful phrases (3 minutes)

Learn these phrases and then test yourself using the cover flap.

May I have a bag, please?	**¿Me da una bolsa, por favor?** *may dah oonah bolsah, por fabor*
Where are the drinks?	**¿Dónde están las bebidas?** *donday estan las bebeedas*
Where is the check-out, please?	**¿Dónde está la caja, por favor?** *donday estah lah kahah, por fabor*
Please key in your PIN.	**Por favor, meta su PIN.** *por fabor, metah soo peen*

5 beauty products

6 dairy products

4 Words to remember (4 minutes)

Learn these words and then test yourself using the cover flap.

bread	**el pan** *el pan*
milk	**la leche** *lah lechay*
butter	**la mantequilla** *lah mantekeeyah*
ham	**el jamón** *el hamon*
salt	**la sal** *lah sal*
pepper	**la pimienta** *lah peemyaintah*
washing powder	**el jabón de lavadora** *el habon day labadorah*
toilet paper	**el papel higiénico** *el papel eehyaineekoh*
nappies	**los pañales** *los panyales*

5 Say it (2 minutes)

Where are the dairy products?

May I have some cheese, please?

Where are the frozen foods?

LA ROPA Y LOS ZAPATOS
Clothes and shoes

Clothes and shoes are measured in metric sizes from 36 upwards. Even allowing for conversion of sizes, Spanish clothes tend to be cut smaller than English ones. Clothes size is **la talla**, but shoe size is **el número**.

2 **Match and repeat** (3 minutes)

Match the numbered items of clothing to the Spanish words in the panel on the left. Test yourself using the cover flap.

❶ **la camisa**
   lah kameesah

❷ **la corbata**
   lah korbatah

❸ **la chaqueta**
   lah chaketah

❹ **el bolsillo**
   el bolseeyoh

❺ **la manga**
   lah mangah

❻ **el pantalón**
   el pantalon

❼ **la falda**
   lah faldah

❽ **las medias**
   las medyas

❾ **los zapatos**
   los thapatos

shirt ❶
tie ❷
jacket ❸
pocket ❹
sleeve ❺
trousers ❻

Cultural tip As in most of mainland Europe, Spain uses the continental system of sizes. Women's clothes sizes usually range from 36 (UK 8, US 6) through to 46 (UK 20, US 18), and shoe sizes from 37 (UK 4, US 5½) to 45 (UK 11, US 12). For men's shirts, a size 41 is a 16-inch collar, 43 is a 17-inch collar, and 45 is an 18-inch collar.

3 Useful phrases (5 minutes)

Practise these phrases and then test yourself using the cover flap.

Do you have a larger size?	**¿Tiene una talla más grande?** *tyenay oonah tayah mas granday*
It's not what I want.	**No es lo que quiero.** *noh es loh kay kyairoh*
I'll take the pink one.	**Me quedo con el rosa.** *may kedoh kon el rrosah*

4 Words to remember (4 minutes)

Colours are adjectives (pp.64–5) and in most cases have a masculine and a feminine form. The feminine is usually formed by substituting an **a** for the final **o**.

red	**rojo/roja** *rrohoh/rrohah*
white	**blanco/blanca** *blankoh/blankah*
blue	**azul** *athool*
yellow	**amarillo/amarilla** *amareeyoh/amareeyah*
green	**verde** *berday*
black	**negro/negra** *negroh/negrah*

— ❼ skirt

— ❽ tights

— ❾ shoes

5 Say it (2 minutes)

What shoe size?

Do you have a black jacket?

Do you have size 38?

Do you have a smaller size?

Respuestas
Answers (Cover with flap)

REPASE Y REPITA
Review and repeat

1 Market

❶ **las alcachofas**
las alka<u>cho</u>fas

❷ **los tomates**
los to<u>ma</u>tes

❸ **los guisantes**
los ghee<u>san</u>tes

❹ **los pimientos**
los peemy<u>ain</u>tos

❺ **las judías**
las hoo<u>dee</u>as

1 Market (3 minutes)

Name the numbered vegetables in Spanish.

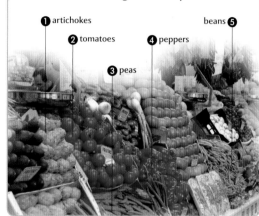

❶ artichokes
❷ tomatoes
❸ peas
❹ peppers
❺ beans

2 Description

❶ The shoes are too expensive.
❷ My room is very small.
❸ I need a softer bed.

2 Description (2 minutes)

What do these sentences mean?

❶ **Los zapatos son demasiados caros.**
❷ **Mi habitación es muy pequeña.**
❸ **Necesito una cama más blanda.**

3 Shops

❶ **la panadería**
lah panadai<u>ree</u>ah

❷ **la joyería**
lah hoyeh<u>ree</u>ah

❸ **la librería**
lah leebrai<u>ree</u>ah

❹ **la pescadería**
lah peskadai<u>ree</u>ah

❺ **la pastelería**
lah pastaylai<u>ree</u>ah

❻ **la carnicería**
lah karneethai<u>ree</u>ah

3 Shops (3 minutes)

Name the numbered shops in Spanish. Then check your answers.

❶ baker
❷ jeweller
❸ bookshop

❹ fishmonger
❺ cake shop
❻ butcher

4 Supermarket (3 minutes)

What is the Spanish for the numbered product categories?

❶ household products

❷ beauty products

❸ drinks

❹ dairy products

❺ frozen foods

4 Supermarket

❶ **los productos del hogar**
los pro*dook*tos del oh*gar*

❷ **los productos de belleza**
los pro*dook*tos day bey*eth*ah

❸ **las bebidas**
las be*bee*das

❹ **los productos lácteos**
los pro*dook*tos *lak*teh-os

❺ **la verdura**
lah ber*door*ah

5 Museum (4 minutes)

Follow this conversation, replying in Spanish following the English prompts.

Buenos días. ¿Qué desean?
❶ I'd like five tickets.

Son setenta y cinco euros.
❷ That's very expensive!

No hacemos descuentos a los niños.
❸ How much is a guide?

Quince euros.
❹ Good. And five tickets, please.

Noventa euros, por favor.
❺ Here you are. Where are the toilets?

A la derecha.
❻ Thank you very much.

5 Museum

❶ **Quisiera cinco entradas.**
kees*yair*ah *theen*koh en*tra*das

❷ **¡Es muy caro!**
es mwee *kar*oh

❸ **¿Cuánto cuesta una guía?**
*kwan*toh *kwes*tah *oo*nah *ghee*ah

❹ **Bien. Y cinco entradas, por favor.**
Byen. ee *theen*koh en*tra*das, por *fa*bor

❺ **Aquí tiene. ¿Dónde están los servicios?**
ah*kee* *tye*nay. *don*day es*tan* los ser*beeth*yos

❻ **Muchas gracias.**
*moo*chas *gra*thyas

1 Warm up (1 minute)

Say "from which platform?" (pp.38-9)

What is the Spanish for the following family members: sister, brother, mother, father, son, and daughter? (pp.10-11)

LAS OCUPACIONES
Jobs

Some occupations have commonly used feminine alternatives - for example, **enfermero** (*male nurse*) and **enfermera** (*female nurse*). Others remain the same. When you describe your occupation, you don't use **un/una** (*a*), saying simply **soy abogado** (*I'm a lawyer*), for example.

2 Words to remember: jobs (7 minutes)

Familiarize yourself with these words and test yourself using the cover flap. The feminine alternative is also shown.

médico *medeekoh*	doctor
dentista *denteestah*	dentist
enfermero/-a *enfermairoh/-ah*	nurse
profesor/-sora *profaysor/-sorah*	teacher
abogado/-a *abogadoh/-ah*	lawyer
contable *kontablay*	accountant
diseñador/-dora *deesenyador/-dorah*	designer
consultor/-a *konsooltor/-ah*	consultant
secretario/-a *sekraytareeoh(-ah)*	secretary
comerciante *komerthyantay*	shopkeeper
electricista *elektreetheestah*	electrician
fontanero/-a *fontanairoh/-ah*	plumber
cocinero/-a *kotheenairoh/-ah*	cook/chef
albañil *albanyeel*	builder
autónomo/-a *aootohnomoh/-ah*	self-employed

Soy fontanero.
soy fontanairoh
I'm a plumber.

Es estudiante.
es estoodyantay
She is a student.

3 Put into practice (4 minutes)

Join in this conversation. Read the Spanish on the left and follow the instructions to form your reply. Then test yourself.

¿Cuál es su profesión?
kw<u>al</u> es soo profesy<u>on</u>

What do you do?

Say: I am a consultant.

Soy consultor.
soy konsool<u>tor</u>

¿Para qué empresa trabaja?
parah kay emp<u>re</u>sah tra<u>ba</u>hah

What company do you work for?

Say: I'm self-employed.

Soy autónomo.
soy aoo<u>toh</u>nomoh

¡Qué interesante!
kay intairays<u>an</u>tay

How interesting!

Say: And what is your profession?

¿Y cuál es su profesión?
ee kw<u>al</u> es soo profesy<u>on</u>

Soy dentista.
soy dent<u>ees</u>tah

I'm a dentist.

Say: My sister is a dentist too.

Mi hermana es dentista también.
mee airr<u>ma</u>nah es dent<u>ees</u>tah tamby<u>en</u>

4 Words to remember: workplace (3 minutes)

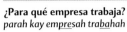

La oficina central está en Madrid.
lah ofee<u>thee</u>nah then<u>tral</u> e<u>stah</u> en ma<u>dreed</u>
Head office is in Madrid.

Familiarize yourself with these words and test yourself.

branch	**la sucursal** *lah sookoor<u>sal</u>*
department	**el departamento** *el departa<u>main</u>toh*
manager	**el jefe** *el <u>he</u>fay*
employee	**el empleado** *el emplay-<u>ah</u>doh*
reception	**la recepción** *lah rrethepthy<u>on</u>*
trainee	**el aprendiz** *el ahpren<u>deeth</u>*

LA OFICINA
The office

An office environment or business situation has its own vocabulary in any language, but there are many items that are virtually universal. Be aware that Spanish computer keyboards have a different layout to the standard English QWERTY convention; they also include **ñ**, vowels with accents, **¡**, and **¿**.

1　Warm up (1 minute)

Practise different ways of introducing yourself in different situations (pp.8-9). Mention your name, occupation (pp. 78-9), and any other information you'd like to volunteer.

2　Words to remember (5 minutes)

Familiarize yourself with these words. Read them aloud several times and try to memorize them. Conceal the Spanish with the cover flap and test yourself.

el monitor *el moneetor*	monitor
el ratón *el rraton*	mouse
el correo electrónico *el korrayoh elektroneekoh*	email
el internet *el eenternet*	internet
la contraseña *lah kontrasenyah*	password
la mensajería de voz *lah mensahereeah day both*	voicemail
el fax *el fax*	fax machine
la fotocopiadora *lah fotokopyadorah*	photocopier
la agenda *lah ah-hendah*	diary
la tarjeta de visita *lah tarhetah day beeseetah*	business card
la reunión *lah reh-oonyon*	meeting
la conferencia *lah konfairentheeah*	conference
el orden del día *el orden del deeah*	agenda

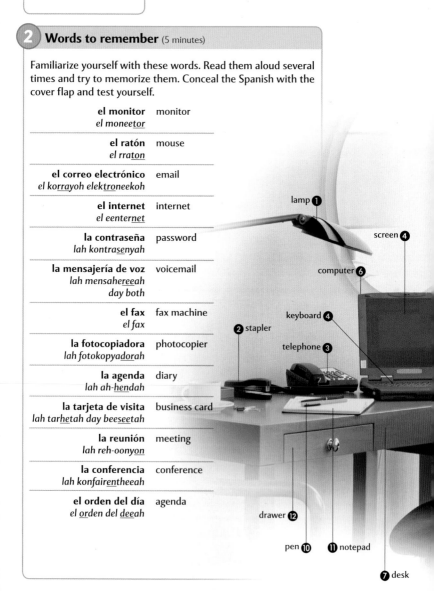

lamp **1**

screen **4**

computer **6**

keyboard **4**

2 stapler

telephone **3**

drawer **12**

pen **10**　**11** notepad

7 desk

3 Useful phrases (2 minutes)

Learn these phrases and then test yourself using the cover flap.

I need to make some photocopies.	**Necesito hacer unas fotocopias.** _netheseetoh ahther oonas fotokopyas_
I'd like to arrange an appointment.	**Quisiera organizar una cita.** _keesyairah organeethar oonah theetah_
I want to send an email.	**Quiero mandar un correo electrónico.** _kyairoh mandar oon korrayoh elektroneekoh_

4 Match and repeat (5 minutes)

Match the numbered items to the Spanish words on the left.

5 Say it (2 minutes)

I'd like to arrange a conference.

I need to send a fax.

Do you have email?

clock **8**

printer **9**

13 swivel chair

❶ **la lámpara**
 lah lamparah

❷ **la grapadora**
 lah grapadohrah

❸ **el teléfono**
 el telefonoh

❹ **la pantalla**
 lah pantayah

❺ **el teclado**
 el tekladoh

❻ **el ordenador**
 el ordenador

❼ **la mesa de escritorio**
 lah mesah day eskreetoryoh

❽ **el reloj**
 el rrelokh

❾ **la impresora**
 lah impresorah

❿ **el bolígrafo**
 el boleegrafoh

⓫ **el bloc**
 el blok

⓬ **el cajón**
 el kahon

⓭ **la silla giratoria**
 lah seeyah heeratoreeah

1 Warm up (1 minute)

Say "library" and "How interesting!" (pp.48-9, pp.78-9)

Ask "What is your profession?" and answer "I'm an engineer". (pp.78-9)

EL MUNDO ACADÉMICO
Academic world

In Spain, students are selected for a first degree (**una licenciatura**) by an average of secondary school grades and an exam. After graduation, some students go on to **un máster** (master's degree) or **un doctora do** (PhD).

2 Useful phrases (3 minutes)

Practise these phrases and then test yourself using the cover flap.

¿Cuál es su especialidad? *kwal es soo espetheeahleedad*	What is your field?
Hago investigación en bioquímica. *ahgoh inbesteegathyon en beeohkeemeekah*	I am doing research in biochemistry.
Soy licenciado en derecho. *soy leethentheeahdoh en derechoh*	I have a degree in law.
Voy a dar una conferencia sobre arquitectura. *boy ah dar oonah konfairayntheeah sobreh arkeetektoorah*	I'm going to give a lecture on architecture.

3 In conversation (5 minutes)

Hola, soy la profesora Fernández.
o-lah, soy lah profaysorah fernandeth

Hello, I'm Professor Fernandez.

¿De qué universidad es usted?
deh keh ooneeberseedad es oosted

What university are you from?

De la Universidad de Murcia.
deh lah ooneeberseedad deh moortheeah

From the University of Murcia.

4 Words to remember (4 minutes)

Familiarize yourself with these words and then test yourself.

Tenemos un stand en la feria.
tenemos oon estand en la fereeah
We have a stand at the trade fair.

conference/lecture	**la conferencia** *lah konfairaintheeah*
trade fair	**la feria** *lah fereeah*
seminar	**el seminario** *el semeenaryoh*
lecture theatre	**el anfiteatro** *el anfeetay-ahtroh*
conference room	**la sala de conferencias** *lah sahlah deh konferaintheeas*
exhibition	**la exposición** *lah eksposeethyon*
library	**la biblioteca** *lah bibleeotekah*
university lecturer	**el profesor de universidad** *el profaysor deh ooneeberseedad*
professor	**el catedrático** *el katedrateekoh*
medicine	**medicina** *medeetheenah*
science	**ciencias** *thyaintheeas*
literature	**literatura** *leetairatoorah*
engineering	**ingeniería** *inhainyaireeah*

5 Say it (2 minutes)

I'm doing research in medicine.

I have a degree in literature.

She's the professor.

¿Cuál es su especialidad?
kwal es soo espethyaleedad

What's your field?

Hago investigación en ingeniería.
ahgoh inbesteegathyon en inhenyaireeah

I'm doing research in engineering.

¡Qué interesante! Yo también.
keh intairaysantay. yoh tambeeayn

How interesting! Me too.

LOS NEGOCIOS
In business

Ask "Can I ...?" (pp.34-5)

Say "I want to send an email". (pp.80-1)

Say "I'd like to arrange an appointment". (pp.80-1)

You will receive a more friendly reception and make a good impression if you make the effort to begin a meeting with a short introduction in Spanish, even if your vocabulary is limited. After that, all parties will probably be happy to continue the proceedings in English.

2 Words to remember (6 minutes)

Familiarize yourself with these words and then test yourself by concealing the Spanish with the cover flap.

el programa *el programah*	schedule
la entrega *lah entraygah*	delivery
el pago *el pahgoh*	payment
el presupuesto *el praysoopwestoh*	budget/ estimate
el precio *el praythyoh*	price
el documento *el dokoomentoh*	document
la factura *lah faktoorah*	invoice
la propuesta *lah propwestah*	proposal
los beneficios *los baynayfeethyos*	profits
las ventas *las bentas*	sales
los números *los noomeros*	figures

el cliente
el klyaintay
client

el informe
el informay
report

Cultural tip A long lunch with wine is still a regular feature of doing business in Spain. As a visiting client you can expect to be taken out to a restaurant, and as a supplier you should consider entertaining your business customers.

3 Useful phrases (6 minutes)

Practise these useful business phrases and then test yourself using the cover flap.

¿Firmamos el contrato?
feer<u>ma</u>mos el kon<u>tra</u>toh
Shall we sign the contract?

el ejecutivo
el eh-hekoo<u>tee</u>boh
executive

el contrato
el kon<u>tra</u>toh
contract

Me manda el contrato, por favor.
may <u>man</u>dah el kon<u>tra</u>toh, por <u>fa</u>bor

Please send me the contract.

¿Hemos acordado un programa?
<u>eh</u>mos akor<u>da</u>doh oon pro<u>gra</u>mah

Have we agreed a schedule?

¿Cuándo puede hacer la entrega?
<u>kwan</u>doh <u>pwe</u>day ah<u>ther</u> lah en<u>tre</u>gah

When can you make the delivery?

¿Cuál es el presupuesto?
<u>kwal</u> es el praysoo<u>pwes</u>toh

What's the budget?

¿Me puede mandar la factura?
may <u>pwe</u>day man<u>dar</u> lah fak<u>too</u>rah

Can you send me the invoice?

4 Say it (2 minutes)

Can you send me the estimate?

Have we agreed a price?

What are the profits?

REPASE Y REPITA
Review and repeat

Respuestas
Answers (Cover with flap)

1 At the office

❶ **la grapadora**
lah grapadorah

❷ **la lámpara**
lah lamparah

❸ **el ordenador**
el ordenador

❹ **el bolígrafo**
el boleegrafoh

❺ **el reloj**
el rrelokh

❻ **el bloc**
el blok

❼ **la mesa de escritorio**
lah mesah day eskreetoryoh

1 At the office (4 minutes)

Name these items.

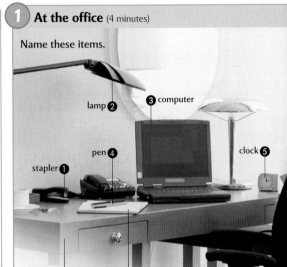

lamp ❷ ❸ computer

pen ❹ clock ❺

stapler ❶

❼ desk ❻ notepad

2 Jobs

❶ **médico**
medeekoh

❷ **fontanero/-a**
fontanairoh/-ah

❸ **comerciante**
komerthyantay

❹ **contable**
kontablay

❺ **estudiante**
estoodyantay

❻ **abogado/-a**
abogadoh/-ah

2 Jobs (3 minutes)

What are these jobs in Spanish?

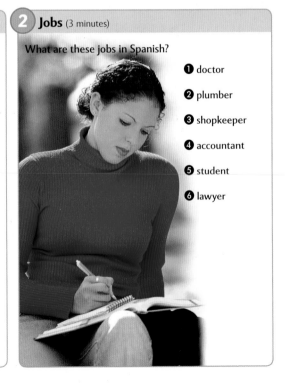

❶ doctor

❷ plumber

❸ shopkeeper

❹ accountant

❺ student

❻ lawyer

3 Work (4 minutes)

Answer these questions following the English prompts.

¿Para qué empresa trabaja?
❶ Say: I am self-employed.

¿En qué universidad está?
❷ Say: I'm at the University of Salamanca.

¿Cuál es su especialidad?
❸ Say: I'm doing research in medicine.

¿Hemos acordado un programa?
❹ Say: Yes, my secretary has the schedule.

3 Work

❶ **Soy autónomo.**
soy aootonomoh

❷ **Estoy en la Universidad de Salamanca.**
estoy en lah ooneeberseedad day salamankah

❸ **Hago investigación en medicina.**
ahgoh inbesteegathyon en medeetheenah

❹ **Sí. mi secretaria tiene el programa.**
see. mee sekretareeah tyenay el programah

4 How much? (4 minutes)

Answer the question with the amount shown in brackets.

❶ ¿Cuánto cuesta el desayuno? (€3.50)

❷ ¿Cuánto cuesta la habitación? (€47)

❸ ¿Cuánto cuesta un kilo de tomates? (€3.25)

❹ ¿Cuánto cuesta un plaza para cuatro noches? (€60)

4 How much?

❶ **Son tres euros cincuenta.**
son tres eh-ooros theenkwentah

❷ **Son cuarenta y siete euros.**
son kwarentah ee seeaytay eh-ooros

❸ **Son tres euros veinticinco.**
son tres eh-ooros beynteetheenkoh

❹ **Son sesenta euros.**
son sesentah eh-ooros

EN LA FARMACIA
At the chemist

1 **Warm up** (1 minute)

Say "I'm allergic to nuts". (pp.24-5)

Say the verb "tener" (to have) in all its forms: yo, tú, él/ella, nosotros(-as), vosotros(-as), ellos (-as). (pp.14-15)

Spanish pharmacists are qualified to give advice and sell over-the-counter medicines, as well as dispense prescription medicines. There is generally a **farmacia de guardia** (*duty pharmacy*) to provide 24-hour service in every town – a list is displayed in every pharmacy.

2 **Match and repeat** (3 minutes)

Match the numbered items to the Spanish words in the panel on the left and test yourself using the cover flap.

1 la venda
lah bendah

2 el jarabe
el harabay

3 las gotas
las gotas

4 la tirita
lah teereetah

5 la jeringuilla
lah hereengheeyah

6 la crema
lah kremah

7 el supositorio
el soopooseetoryoh

8 la pastilla
lah pasteeyah

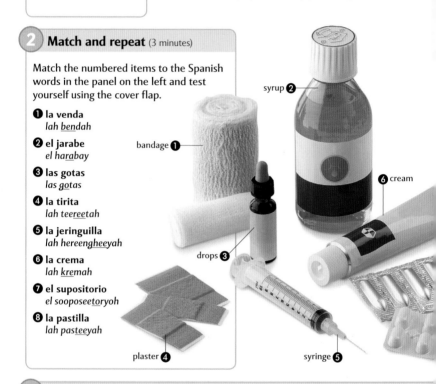

syrup **2**

bandage **1**

6 cream

drops **3**

plaster **4**

syringe **5**

3 **In conversation** (3 minutes)

**Buenos días, señor.
¿Qué desea?**
*bwenos deeyas, senyor.
kay desayah*

Good morning, sir. What would you like?

Tengo dolor de estómago.
tengoh dolor day estomagoh

I have a stomach ache.

¿Tiene diarrea?
tyenay deeahrrayah

Do you have diarrhoea?

4 **Words to remember** (2 minutes)

Familiarize yourself with these words and test yourself using the cover flap.

Tengo dolor de cabeza.
tengoh dolor day kabethah

I have a headache.

headache	**el dolor de cabeza** *el dolor day kabethah*
stomach ache	**el dolor de estómago** *el dolor day estomagoh*
diarrhoea	**la diarrea** *lah deeahrrayah*
cold	**el resfriado** *el rresfreeahdoh*
cough	**la tos** *lah tos*
sunstroke	**la insolación** *lah eensolatheeyon*
toothache	**el dolor de muelas** *el dolor day mwelas*

6 **Say it** (2 minutes)

I have a cold.

Do you have that as a cream?

He has toothache.

7 suppository

8 tablet

5 **Useful phrases** (4 minutes)

Practise these phrases and then test yourself using the cover flap.

I have sunstroke.	**Tengo una insolación.** *tengoh oonah eensolatheeyon*
Do you have that as a syrup?	**¿Lo tiene en jarabe?** *loh tyenay en harabay*
I'm allergic to penicillin.	**Soy alérgico a la penicilina.** *soy alerheekoh ah lah peneetheeleenah*

No, pero tengo dolor de cabeza.
noh, peroh tengoh dolor day kabethah

No, but I have a headache.

Aquí tiene.
ahkee tyenay

Here you are.

¿Lo tiene en pastilla?
loh tyenay en pasteeyah

Do you have this as pills?

EL CUERPO
The body

Say "I have a toothache" and "I have a sunstroke". (pp.88-9)

Say the Spanish for "red", "green", "black", and "yellow". (pp.74-5)

You are most likely to need to refer to parts of the body in the context of illness - for example, when describing aches and pains to a doctor. The most common phrases for talking about discomfort are **Tengo un dolor en la/el...** (*I have a pain in the...*) and **Me duele la/el...** (*My ... hurts me*).

2 **Match and repeat: body** (6 minutes)

Match the numbered parts of the body with the list on the left. Test yourself by using the cover flap.

1 la mano
lah manoh

2 la cabeza
lah kabethah

3 el hombro
el ombroh

4 el codo
el kodoh

5 el pelo
el peloh

6 el brazo
el brathoh

7 el cuello
el kweyoh

8 el pecho
el pechoh

9 el estómago
el estomagoh

10 la pierna
lah pyairnah

11 la rodilla
lah rrodeeyah

12 el pie
el pee-ay

1 hand
4 elbow
5 hair
2 head
6 arm
shoulder **3**
7 neck
chest **8**
stomach **9**
leg **10**
knee **11**
12 foot

3 Match and repeat: face (3 minutes)

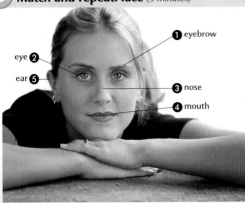

❶ eyebrow

eye ❷

ear ❺

❸ nose

❹ mouth

Match the numbered facial features with the list on the right.

❶ **la ceja**
lah thayah

❷ **el ojo**
el oh-hoh

❸ **la nariz**
lah nareeth

❹ **la boca**
lah bokah

❺ **la oreja**
lah ohrayah

4 Useful phrases (3 minutes)

Learn these phrases and then test yourself using the cover flap.

I have a pain in my back.	**Tengo un dolor en la espalda.** *tengoh oon dolor en lah espalda*
I have a rash on my arm.	**Tengo un sarpullido en el brazo.** *tengoh oon sarpooyeedoh en el brathoh*
I don't feel well.	**No me encuentro bien.** *noh may enkwentroh byen*

5 Put into practice (2 minutes)

Join in this conversation and test yourself using the cover flap.

¿Cuál es el problema?
kwal es el problemah

What's the problem?

Say: I don't feel well.

No me encuentro bien.
noh may enkwentroh byen

¿Dónde le duele?
donday lay dwelay

Where does it hurt?

Say: I have a pain in the shoulder.

Tengo un dolor en el hombro.
tengoh oon dolor en el ombroh

1 Warm up (1 minute)

Say "I need some tablets". (pp.60-1, pp.88-9)

Say "He needs some cream". (pp.88-9)

What is the Spanish for "I don't have a son". (pp.10-15)

EN EL MÉDICO
At the doctor

Unless it's an emergency, you have to book an appointment with the doctor and pay when you leave. You can usually reclaim the money if you have medical insurance. Your hotel, a local pharmacy, or a tourist information office may be able to tell you the names and addresses of local doctors.

2 Useful phrases you may hear (3 minutes)

Practise these phrases and then test yourself using the cover flap to conceal the Spanish on the left.

No es grave. *noh es gravay*	It's not serious.
Necesita hacerse unas pruebas. *netheseetah ahthersay oonas prwaybas*	You need to have some tests.
Tiene una infección de riñón. *tyenay oonah infekthyon day rreenyon*	You have a kidney infection.
Necesita ir al hospital. *netheseetah eer al ospeetal*	You need to go to hospital.

Le voy a dar una receta.
lay boy ah dar oonah rrethetah
I'm going to give you a prescription.

3 In conversation (5 minutes)

¿Cuál es el problema?
kwal es el problemah

What's the problem?

Tengo un dolor en el pecho.
tengoh oon dolor en el pechoh

I have a pain in my chest.

Déjeme que la examine.
dayhaymay kay lah eksameenay

Let me examine you.

4 **Useful phrases you may need to say** (4 minutes)

Practise these phrases and then test yourself using the cover flap.

I am diabetic.	**Soy diabético/-a.** *soy deeah<u>be</u>teekoh/-ah*
I am epileptic.	**Soy epiléptico/-a.** *soy epee<u>lep</u>teekoh/-ah*
I'm asthmatic.	**Soy asmático/-a.** *soy a<u>sma</u>teekoh/-ah*
I have a heart condition.	**Tengo un problema de corazón.** *<u>ten</u>goh oon pro<u>ble</u>mah day korathon*
I have a temperature.	**Tengo fiebre.** *<u>ten</u>goh <u>fyay</u>bray*
I feel faint.	**Estoy mareado.** *es<u>toy</u> maray-<u>ah</u>doh*
It's urgent.	**Es urgente.** *es oor<u>hen</u>tay*

Estoy embarazada.
es<u>toy</u> embara<u>tha</u>dah
I am pregnant.

Conversational tip
If you are an EU national, you are entitled to free emergency medical treatment in Spain on production of a European Health Insurance Card or an E111 form. For an ambulance, call 112.

5 **Say it** (2 minutes)

My son is diabetic.

I have a pain in my arm.

It's not urgent.

¿Es grave?
es <u>gra</u>vay

Is it serious?

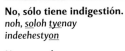

No, sólo tiene indigestión.
noh, <u>so</u>loh <u>tye</u>nay indeehesty<u>on</u>

No, you only have indigestion.

¡Menos mal!
<u>may</u>nos mal

What a relief!

EN EL HOSPITAL
At the hospital

1 Warm up (1 minute)

Say "How long is the journey?" (pp.42-3)

Ask "Is is serious?" (pp.92-3)

What is the Spanish for "mouth" and "head"? (pp.90-1)

It is useful to know a few basic phrases relating to hospitals and medical treatment for use in an emergency, or in case you need to visit a friend or colleague in hospital. Most Spanish hospitals have only two beds per room and their own en-suite bathroom facilities.

2 Useful phrases (5 minutes)

Familiarize yourself with these phrases. Conceal the Spanish with the cover flap and test yourself.

¿Cuáles son las horas de visita? _kwales son las oras day beeseetah_	What are the visiting hours?
¿Cuánto tiempo va a tardar? _kwantoh tyempoh bah ah tardar_	How long will it take?
¿Va a doler? _bah ah doler_	Will it hurt?
Túmbese aquí por favor. _toombesay ahkee por fabor_	Please lie down here.
No puede comer nada. _noh pweday komer nadah_	You cannot eat anything.
No mueva la cabeza. _noh mwebah lah kabethah_	Don't move your head.
Abra la boca por favor. _ahbrah lah bokah por fabor_	Please open your mouth.
Necesita un análisis de sangre. _netheseetah oon analeesees day sangray_	You need a blood test.

¿Dónde está la sala de espera?
donday estah lah salah day esperah
Where is the waiting room?

el gotero
el goteroh
drip

¿Se encuentra mejor?
say enkwentrah mehor
Are you feeling better?

3 Words to remember (4 minutes)

Su radiografía es normal.
soo rradyografeeah es normal
Your x-ray is normal.

Familiarize yourself with these words and test yourself using the cover flap.

emergency department	**el servicio de urgencias** *el serbeethyoh day oorhentheeas*
x-ray department	**el servicio de radiología** *el serbeethyoh day rradyoloheeah*
children's ward	**la sala de pediatría** *lah salah day pedeeatreeah*
operating theatre	**el quirófano** *el keerofanoh*
waiting room	**la sala de espera** *lah salah day esperah*
stairs	**las escaleras** *las eskaleras*

4 Put into practice (3 minutes)

Join in this conversation. Cover up the text on the right and complete the anwering part of the dialogue in Spanish. Check your answers and repeat if necessary.

Tiene una infección.
tyenay oonah infekthyon

You have an infection.

Ask: Do I need tests?

¿Necesito hacerme pruebas?
netheseetoh ahthermay prwaybas

Primero necesita un análisis de sangre.
preemeroh netheseetah oon analeesees day sangray

First you will need a blood test.

Ask: Will it hurt?

¿Me va a doler?
may bah ah doler

5 Say it (2 minutes)

Does he need a blood test?

Where is the children's ward?

Do I need an x-ray?

No, no se preocupe.
noh, noh say pray-okoopay

No. Don't worry.

Ask: How long will it take?

¿Cuánto tiempo va a tardar?
kwantoh tyempoh bah ah tardar

REPASE Y REPITA
Review and repeat

Respuestas
Answers (Cover with flap)

1 The body

❶ la cabeza
lah kabethah

❷ el brazo
el brathoh

❸ el pecho
el pechoh

❹ el estómago
el estomagoh

❺ la pierna
lah pyairnah

❻ la rodilla
lah rrodeeyah

❼ el pie
el pee-ay

1 The body (4 minutes)

Name the numbered body parts in Spanish.

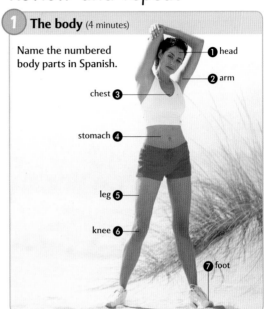

- ❶ head
- ❷ arm
- chest ❸
- stomach ❹
- leg ❺
- knee ❻
- ❼ foot

2 On the phone

❶ Quisiera hablar con Ana Flores.
keesyairah hablar kon anna flores

❷ Luis Cortés de Don Frío.
looees kortes day don free-oh

❸ ¿Puedo dejar un mensaje?
pwedoh dehar oon mensahay

❹ La cita el lunes a las once está bien.
lah theetah el loones ah las onthay estah byen

❺ Gracias, adiós.
grathyas, addy-os

2 On the phone (4 minutes)

You are arranging an appointment. Follow the conversation, replying in Spanish following the English prompts.

Dígame, Apex Finanzas.
❶ I'd like to speak to Ana Flores.

¿De parte de quién?
❷ Luis Cortés, of Don Frío.

Lo siento, está comunicando.
❸ Can I leave a message?

Sí, dígame.
❹ The appointment on Monday at 11am is fine.

Muy bien, adiós.
❺ Thank you, goodbye.

3 Clothing (3 minutes)

Say the Spanish words for the numbered items of clothing.

tie ❶

❷ jacket

❹ skirt

trousers ❸

❻ tights

shoes ❺

3 Clothing

❶ **la corbata**
lah korbatah

❷ **la chaqueta**
lah chaketah

❸ **el pantalón**
el pantalon

❹ **la falda**
lah faldah

❺ **los zapatos**
los thapatos

❻ **las medias**
las medeeas

4 At the doctor's (4 minutes)

Say these phrases in Spanish.

❶ I don't feel well.
❷ I have a heart condition.
❸ Do I need to go to hospital?
❹ I am pregnant.

4 At the doctor's

❶ **No me encuentro bien.**
noh may enkwentroh byen

❷ **Tengo un problema de corazón.**
tengoh oon problemah day korathon

❸ **¿Necesito ir al hospital?**
netheseetoh eer al ospeetal

❹ **Estoy embarazada.**
estoy embarathadah

EN CASA
At home

1 **Warm up** (1 minute)

Say the months of the year in Spanish. (pp.28-9)

Ask "Is there a car park?" and "Are there toilets?" (pp.48-9 and pp.62-3)

Many city-dwellers live in apartment blocks (**edificios**), but in rural areas the houses tend to be detached (**chalet**). If you want to know how big it is you will need to ask in square metres. If you want to know how many bedrooms there are ask **¿Cuántos dormitorios hay?**.

2 **Match and repeat** (5 minutes)

Match the numbered items to the list and test yourself using the flap.

❶ **la chimenea**
  lah cheemenayah

❷ **la ventana**
  lah bentanah

❸ **el tejado**
  el tehadoh

❹ **la terraza**
  lah terratha

❺ **la persiana**
  lah perseeanah

❻ **el muro**
  el mooroh

❼ **la puerta**
  lah pwertah

❽ **el garaje**
  el garahay

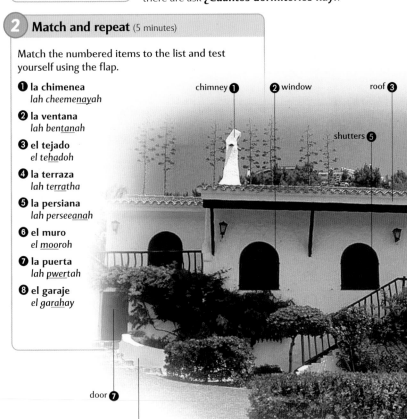

chimney ❶   ❷ window   roof ❸

shutters ❺

door ❼

wall ❻

Cultural tip You almost never see a Spanish home without shutters at every window. These are closed at night and often during the heat of the day in summer. Curtains, where they exist at all, tend to be more for decoration. Carpets are not popular in Spanish homes; ceramic tiles or parquet floors with rugs are a more common flooring solution.

3 Words to remember (4 minutes)

¿Cuánto es el alquiler al mes?
kwantoh es el alkeeler al mes
What is the rent per month?

Familiarize yourself with these words and test yourself using the cover flap.

room	**la habitación**	*lah abeetathyon*
floor	**el suelo**	*el sweloh*
ceiling	**el techo**	*el techoh*
bedroom	**el dormitorio**	*el dormeetoreeoh*
bathroom	**el cuarto de baño**	*el kwartoh day banyoh*
kitchen	**la cocina**	*lah kotheenah*
dining room	**el comedor**	*el komedor*
living room	**el cuarto de estar**	*el kwartoh day estar*
cellar	**el sótano**	*el sotahnoh*
attic	**el ático**	*el ahteekoh*

terrace ❹

garage ❽

4 Put into practice (3 minutes)

Practise these phrases and test yourself.

¿Hay un garaje?
ah-ee oon garahay

Is there a garage?

¿Cuándo está disponible?
kwandoh estah deesponeeblay

When is it available?

MAY MAI MAI MEI

¿Está amueblado?
estah amwebladoh

Is it furnished?

5 Say it (2 minutes)

Is there a dining room?

Is it large?

Is it available in July?

1 Warm up (1 minute)

What is the Spanish for "table", "chair", "toilet(s)", and "curtains"? (pp.20-1, pp.80-1, pp.52-3, pp.60-1)

Say "beautiful", "soft", and "big". (pp.64-5)

EN LA CASA
Inside the house

If you're renting a holiday house or villa in Spain, the most usual option is to take it for a full month or, if not, for a **quincena**, the first or last fifteen days of the month. You will need to check in advance whether the cost of utilities is included in the rent. Most holiday homes have no telephone.

2 Match and repeat (3 minutes)

Match the numbered items to the list in the panel on the left. Then test yourself by concealing the Spanish with the cover flap.

1 la encimera
lah entheemerah

2 el fregadero
el fregaderoh

3 el microondas
el meekro-ondas

4 el horno
el ornoh

5 la cocina
lah kotheenah

6 el frigorífico
el freegoreefeekoh

7 la mesa
lah mesah

8 la silla
lah seeyah

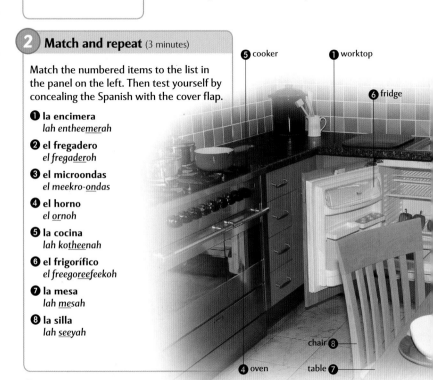

5 cooker 1 worktop

6 fridge

chair 8

4 oven table 7

3 In conversation (3 minutes)

Este es el horno.
estay es el ornoh

This is the oven.

¿Hay también un lavavajillas?
ah-ee tambyen oon lababaheeyas

Is there a dishwasher as well?

Sí, y hay un congelador grande.
see, ee ah-ee oon konhelador granday

Yes, and there's a big freezer.

4 **Words to remember** (2 minutes)

Familiarize yourself with these words and test yourself using the cover flap.

El sofá es nuevo.
el sofah es nweboh
The sofa is new.

wardrobe	**el armario**
	el armaryoh
sofa	**el sofá**
	el sofah
fireplace	**la chimenea**
	lah cheemenayah
carpet	**la moqueta**
	lah moketah
bath	**la bañera**
	lah banyerah
toilet	**el váter**
	el bater
wash basin	**el lavabo**
	el lababoh

❷ sink   microwave ❸

5 **Useful phrases** (4 minutes)

Practise these phrases and then test yourself.

The cooker is broken.	**La cocina no funciona.**
	lah kotheenah
	noh foonthyonah
I don't like the curtains.	**No me gustan las cortinas.**
	noh may goostan
	las korteenas
Is electricity included?	**¿Está incluida la electricidad?**
	estah eenklooeedah
	lah ehektreetheedad

6 **Say it** (2 minutes)

Is there a microwave?

I like the fireplace.

What a soft sofa!

Todo está muy nuevo.
todoh estah mwee nweboh

Everything is very new.

Y aquí está la lavadora.
ee ahkee estah lah labadorah

And here's the washing machine.

¡Qué azulejos más bonitos!
kay ah-thoolayhos mas boneetos

What beautiful tiles!

EL JARDÍN
The garden

1 Warm up (1 minute)

Say "I need" and "you need". (pp.64-5, pp.92-4)

What is the Spanish for "day" and "month"? (pp.28-9)

Say the days of the week. (pp.28-9)

The garden of a house or a villa may be communal, or at least partly shared. Check with the estate agent or rental agent carefully to establish the position. In some cases, a charge for upkeep of the garden may be included with the rent of an apartment. Check with the agent.

2 Words to remember (3 minutes)

Familiarize yourself with these words and test yourself using the cover flap.

la máquina cortacésped *lah makeenah kortathesped*	lawn mower
la horca *lah orkah*	fork
la pala *lah palah*	spade
el rastrillo *el rrastreeyoh*	rake
el vivero *el beeberoh*	garden centre

terrace **1**

tree **2**

flowers **7**

8 weeds

soil **3**

path **9**

3 Useful phrases (4 minutes)

Practise these phrases and then test yourself using the cover flap.

The gardener comes once a week.	**El jardinero viene una vez a la semana.** *el hardeenairoh byainay oonah beth ah lah semanah*
Can you mow the lawn?	**¿Puede cortar el césped?** *pweday kortar el thesped*
Is the garden private?	**¿Es el jardín privado?** *es el hardeen preebadoh*
The garden needs watering.	**El jardín necesita que lo rieguen.** *el hardeen netheseetah kay loh rreeayghen*

❺ hedge
❹ lawn

4 Words to remember (5 minutes)

Match the numbered items to the words in the panel on the right.

❶ **la terraza** *lah terrathah*
❷ **el árbol** *el arbol*
❸ **la tierra** *lah tyairrah*
❹ **el césped** *el thesped*
❺ **el seto** *el setoh*
❻ **las plantas** *las plantas*
❼ **las flores** *las flores*
❽ **las malas hierbas** *las malas yerbas*
❾ **el camino** *el kameenoh*
❿ **el parterre** *el partairray*

❻ plants
❿ flowerbed

5 Say it (2 minutes)

The lawn needs water.

Are there any trees?

The gardener comes on Fridays.

LOS ANIMALES DE COMPAÑÍA
Pets

1 **Warm up** (1 minute)

Say "My name's …".
(pp.8-9)

Say "Don't worry".
(pp.94-5)

What's "your" in Spanish?
(pp.12-13)

"Pet passports" are now available to enable holiday-makers and commuters to take their pets with them to Spain and avoid quarantine on return to the UK. Consult your vet for details on the necessary vaccinations and paperwork.

2 **Match and repeat** (3 minutes)

Match the numbered animals to the Spanish words in the panel on the left. Then test yourself using the cover flap.

❶ **el gato**
el gatoh

❷ **el conejo**
el konehoh

❸ **el pájaro**
el paharoh

❹ **el pez**
el peth

❺ **el perro**
el perroh

❻ **el hámster**
el hamster

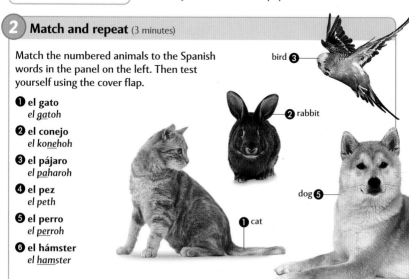

bird ❸

❷ rabbit

dog ❺

❶ cat

3 **Useful phrases** (4 minutes)

Learn these phrases and then test yourself using the cover flap.

¿Es bueno el perro? *es bwenoh el perroh*	Is this dog friendly?
¿Puedo llevar el perro? *pwedoh yebar el perroh*	Can I bring my dog?
Me dan miedo los gatos. *may dan myaydoh los gatos*	I'm frightened of cats.
Mi perro no muerde. *mee perroh noh mweday*	My dog doesn't bite.

Este gato está lleno de pulgas.
estay gatoh estah yenoh day poolgas
This cat is full of fleas.

Cultural tip Many dogs in Spain are working or guard dogs and you may encounter them tethered or roaming free. Approach farms and rural houses with particular care. Look out for warning notices such as **¡Cuidado con el perro!** (*Beware of the dog*).

¡CUIDADO CON EL PERRO!

Mi perro no está bien.
mee perroh noh estah byen
My dog is not well.

hamster ⑥

fish ④

4 Words to remember (4 minutes)

Familiarize yourself with these words and test yourself using the cover flap.

basket	**la cesta**	*lah thestah*
cage	**la jaula**	*lah haoolah*
bowl	**el bol**	*el bol*
collar	**el collar**	*el koyar*
lead	**la correa**	*lah korray-ah*
vet	**el veterinario**	*el betereenaryoh*
vaccination	**la vacuna**	*lah bakoonah*
pet passport	**el pasaporte de animales**	*el pasaportay day aneemales*
flea spray	**el spray antipulgas**	*el espraee anteepoolgas*

5 Put into practice (3 minutes)

Join in this conversation. Read the Spanish on the left and follow the instructions to make your reply. Then test yourself by concealing the answers with the cover flap.

¿Es suyo este perro?
es sooyoh estay perroh

Is this your dog?

Say: Yes, he's called Sandy.

Sí, se llama Sandy.
see, say yamah Sandy

Me dan miedo los perros.
may dan myaydoh los perros

I'm frightened of dogs.

Say: Don't worry. He's friendly.

No se preocupe. Es bueno.
noh say prayohkoopay. es bwenoh

Respuestas
Answers (Cover with flap)

REPASE Y REPITA
Review and repeat

1 Colours

❶ **negra**
negrah

❷ **pequeños**
pekenyos

❸ **rojo**
rrohoh

❹ **verde**
berday

❺ **amarillos**
amareeyos

1 Colours (4 minutes)

Complete the sentences with the Spanish word for the colour in brackets. Watch out for masculine and feminine.

❶ Quisiera la camisa _____. (black)

❷ Estos zapatos son muy _____. (small)

❸ ¿Tiene este traje en _____? (red)

❹ No, pero lo tengo en _____. (green)

❺ Quiero los zapatos _____. (yellow)

2 Kitchen

❶ **la cocina**
lah kotheenah

❷ **el frigorífico**
el freegoreefeekoh

❸ **el fregadero**
el fregaderoh

❹ **el microondas**
el meekro-ondas

❺ **el horno**
el ornoh

❻ **la silla**
lah seeyah

❼ **la mesa**
lah mesah

2 Kitchen (4 minutes)

Say the Spanish words for the numbered items.

cooker ❶   fridge ❷

❺ oven   chair ❻

3 House (4 minutes)

You are visiting a house in Spain. Join in the conversation, asking questions in Spanish following the English prompts.

Éste es el cuarto de estar.
❶ What a lovely fireplace.

Sí, y tiene una cocina muy grande.
❷ How many bedrooms are there?

Hay tres dormitorios.
❸ Do you have a garage?

Sí, pero no hay un jardín.
❹ When is it available?

En julio.
❺ What is the rent a month?

3 House

❶ ¡Qué chimenea
más bonita!
kay cheemen_ayah_
mas bon_ee_tah

❷ ¿Cuántos
dormitorios hay?
kw_antos_
dormee_toreeos_
ah-ee

❸ ¿Tiene garaje?
t_ye_nay ga_ra_hay

❹ ¿Cuándo está
disponible?
kw_andoh estah
deespon_ee_blay

❺ ¿Cuánto es el
alquiler al mes?
kw_antoh_ es el alkee_ler
al mes

4 At home (3 minutes)

microwave **❹**

❸ sink

table **❼**

Say the Spanish for the following items.

❶ washing machine
❷ sofa
❸ attic
❹ dining room
❺ tree
❻ garden

4 At home

❶ la lavadora
lah laba_dora_h

❷ el sofá
el sof_ah_

❸ el ático
el _ah_teekoh

❹ el comedor
el kome_dor_

❺ el árbol
el _ar_bol

❻ el jardín
el har_deen_

EL BANCO Y LA OFICINA DE CORREOS
Bank and post office

1 Warm up (1 minute)

Ask "How do I get to the bank?" and "How do I get to the post office?" (pp.50-1)

What's the Spanish for "passport"? (pp.54-5)

How do you ask "What time is the meeting?" (pp.30-1)

Banks and post offices usually open only until lunchtime (approximately 2pm) and are generally closed at weekends. **Cajas de ahorros** (*savings banks*) have different hours. In summer, operation times may be shorter.

2 Words to remember: post (3 minutes)

los sellos *los seyos*	stamps
la postal *lah postal*	postcard
el paquete *el paketay*	parcel
por avión *por abyon*	by air mail
el correo certificado *el korrayoh therteefeekadoh*	registered post
el buzón *el boothon*	post box
el código postal *el kodeegoh postal*	postcode
el cartero *el kartairoh*	postman

Familiarize yourself with these words and test yourself using the cover flap to conceal the Spanish on the left.

el sobre
el sobray
envelope

¿Cuánto es para el Reino Unido?
kwantoh es parah el rrayeenoh ooneedoh
How much is it for the United Kingdom?

3 In conversation (3 minutes)

Quisiera sacar dinero.
keesyairah sakar deeneroh

I'd like to withdraw some money.

¿Tiene identificación?
tyenay eedenteefeekathyon

Do you have any ID?

Sí, aquí tiene mi pasaporte.
see, ahkee tyenay mee pasaportay

Yes, here's my passport.

¿Cómo puedo pagar?
komoh pwedoh pagar
How can I pay?

4 Words to remember: bank (2 minutes)

Familiarize yourself with these words and test yourself using the cover flap to cover the Spanish on the right.

PIN	**el pin** *el peen*
bank	**el banco** *el bankoh*
cashier	**el cajero** *el kaheroh*
cashpoint/ATM	**el cajero automático** *el kaheroh aootomateekoh*
notes	**los billetes** *los beeyetes*
travellers' cheques	**los cheques de viaje** *los chekes day beeahay*

5 Useful phrases (4 minutes)

Practise these phrases and then test yourself using the cover flap.

I'd like to change some money.	**Quisiera cambiar dinero.** *keesyairah kambyar deeneroh*
What is the exchange rate?	**¿A cuánto está el cambio?** *ah kwantoh estah el kambyoh*
I'd like to withdraw some money.	**Quisiera sacar dinero.** *keesyairah sakar deeneroh*

6 Say it (2 minutes)

I'd like to change some travellers' cheques.

Do I need my passport?

I'd like a stamp for the United Kingdom.

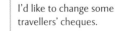

Meta su pin, por favor.
metah soo peen, por fabor

Please key in your PIN.

¿Tengo que firmar también?
tengoh kay feermar tambyen

Do I have to sign as well?

No, no hace falta.
noh, noh ahthay faltah

No, that's not necessary.

1 Warm up (1 minute)

What is the Spanish for "doesn't work"? (pp.60-1)

What's the Spanish for "today" and "tomorrow"? (pp.28-9)

LOS SERVICIOS
Services

You can combine the Spanish words on these pages with the vocabulary you learned in week 10 to help you explain basic problems and cope with arranging most repairs. When organizing construction work or a repair, it's a good idea to agree to the price and method of payment in advance.

2 Words to remember (4 minutes)

Familiarize yourself with these words and test yourself using the cover flap.

el fontanero *el fontanairoh*	plumber
el electricista *el ehlektreetheestah*	electrician
el mecánico *el mekaneekoh*	mechanic
el albañil *el albanyeel*	builder
la asistenta *lah aseestentah*	cleaner
el pintor *el peentor*	decorator
el carpintero *el karpeenteroh*	carpenter
el técnico *el tekneekoh*	technician

la llave de tuercas
lah yabay day twerkas
wheel brace

No necesito un mecánico.
noh netheseetoh oon mekaneekoh
I don't need a mechanic.

3 In conversation (3 minutes)

La lavadora no funciona.
lah labadorah noh foothyonah

The washing machine's not working.

Sí, la manguera está rota.
see, lah mangherah estah rrotah

Yes, the hose is broken.

¿La puede arreglar?
lah pweday arreglar

Can you repair it?

4 Useful phrases (3 minutes)

¿Dónde me pueden arreglar la plancha?
donday may pweden arreglar lah planchah
Where can I get the iron repaired?

Practise these phrases and then test yourself using the cover flap.

Can you clean the bathroom?	**¿Puede limpiar el cuarto de baño?** *pweday leempyar el kwartoh day banyoh*
Can you repair the boiler?	**¿Puede arreglar la caldera?** *pweday arreglar lah kalderah*
Do you know a good electrician?	**¿Conoce a un buen electricista?** *konothay ah oon ehlektreetheestah*

5 Put into practice (4 minutes)

Empiezo el trabajo mañana.
empyaythoh el trabahoh manyanah
I start the job tomorrow.

los planos
los planos
plans

Practise these phrases. Cover the text on the right and complete the dialogue in Spanish. Check your answers and repeat if necessary.

Su verja está rota. *soo berhah estah rrotah* Your gate is broken. Ask: Do you know a good builder?	**¿Conoce a un buen albañil?** *konothay ah oon bwen albanyeel*
Sí, hay uno en el pueblo. *see, ah-ee oonoh en el pwebloh* Yes, there is one in the village. Ask: Do you have his phone number?	**¿Tiene su número de teléfono?** *tyenay soo noomeroh day telefonoh*

No, va a necesitar una nueva.
noh, bah ah netheseetar oonah nwebah

No, you'll need a new one.

¿Lo puede hacer hoy?
loh pweday ahther oy

Can you do it today?

No, volveré mañana.
noh, bolberay manyanah

No. I'll come back tomorrow.

1 Warm up (1 minute)

Say the days of the week in Spanish. (pp.28-9)

How do you say "cleaner"? (pp.110-11)

Say "It's 9.30", "10.45", "12.00". (pp.30-1)

VENIR
To come

The verb **venir** (*to come*) is one of the most useful verbs. As well as the main verb (see below) it is worth knowing the instruction **¡ven!/¡venga!** (*come here!* informal/formal). Note that *with me* becomes **conmigo** and *with you* **contigo**: **ven conmigo** (*come with me*); **vengo contigo** (*I'm going with you*).

2 Venir: to come (6 minutes)

Say the different forms of the verb aloud, reading from the table. Use the cover flap to test yourself and, when you are confident, practise the sample sentences below.

Vienen en muchos colores.
beeaynen en moochos kolores
They come in many colours.

yo vengo *yoh bengoh*	I come
tú vienes/usted viene *too byenes/oosted byenay*	you come (informal/ formal singular)
él/ella viene *el/eh-yah byenay*	he/she comes
nosotros(-as) venimos *nosotros(-as) beneemos*	we come
vosotros(-as) venís *bosotros(-as) benees*	you come (informal plural)
ustedes vienen *oostedes byenen*	you come (formal plural)
ellos/ellas vienen *eh-yos/eh-yas byenen*	they come
Vengo ahora. *bengoh ah-orah*	I'm coming now.
Venimos todos los martes. *beneemos todos los martes*	We come every Tuesday.
Vienen en tren. *byenen en tren*	They come by train.

Conversational tip To say *I come from England* in Spanish, you have to use the verb *to be*, as in **soy inglés** (*I am from England*). When you use the verb *to come*, as in **Vengo de Londres**, it means you have just arrived from London.

3 Useful phrases (4 minutes)

Learn these phrases and then test yourself using the cover flap.

When can I come?	**¿Cuándo puedo venir?** _kwandoh pwedoh beneer_
Does it come in size 44?	**¿Viene en la talla 44?** _byenay en lah tayah kwarentah ee kwatroh_
The cleaner comes every Monday.	**La asistenta viene todos los lunes.** _lah aseestentah byenay todos los loones_
Come with me. (informal/formal)	**Ven conmigo/ Venga conmigo.** _ben konmeegoh/ bengah konmeegoh_

¿Puede venir el viernes?
pweday beneer el byairnes
Can you come on Friday?

4 Put into practice (4 minutes)

Practise these phrases. Then cover the text on the right and say the anwering part of the dialogue in Spanish. Check your answers and repeat if necessary.

Peluquería Cristina, dígame.
pelookereeah kristeenah, deegamay

Christine's hair salon. Can I help you?

Say: I'd like an appointment.

Quisiera una cita.
keesyairah oonah theetah

¿Cuándo quiere venir?
kwandoh kyairay beneer

When do you want to come?

Say: Today, if possible.

Hoy, si es posible.
oy, see es poseeblay

Sí, claro. ¿A qué hora?
see klaroh, ah kay orah

Yes of course. What time?

Say: At 10.30.

A las diez y media.
ah las dyeth ee medeeah

LA POLICÍA Y EL DELITO
Police and crime

What's the Spanish for "big" and "small"? (pp.64-5)

Say "The room is big" and "The bed is small". (pp.64-5)

While in Spain, if you are the victim of a crime, you should go to the police station to report it, or in an emergency, you can dial 112. You may have to explain your complaint in Spanish, so some basic vocabulary is useful.

2 Words to remember: crime (4 minutes)

Familiarize yourself with these words.

Necesito un abogado.
netheseetoh oon abogadoh
I need a lawyer.

el robo *el rroboh*	robbery
la denuncia *lah denoontheeah*	police report
el ladrón *el ladron*	thief
la policía *lah poleetheeah*	police
la declaración *lah deklarathyon*	statement
el testigo *el testeegoh*	witness
el abogado *el abogadoh*	lawyer

3 Useful phrases (3 minutes)

Learn these phrases and then test yourself.

Me han robado. *may an rrobadoh*	I've been robbed.
¿Qué han robado? *kay an rrobadoh*	What was stolen?
¿Vió quién lo hizo? *byoh kyain loh eethoh*	Did you see who did it?
¿Cuándo ocurrió? *kwandoh okoorryoh*	When did it happen?

la cámara de fotos
lah kamarah day fotos
camera

la cartera
la karterah
purse

4 Words to remember: appearance (5 minutes)

Learn these words. Remember some adjectives have a feminine form.

Él es bajo y tiene bigote.
el es bahoh ee tyenay beegotay
He is short and has a moustache.

Tiene el pelo negro y corto.
tyenay el peloh negroh ee kortoh
He has short, black hair.

man	**el hombre** *el ombray*
woman	**la mujer** *lah moo-hair*
tall	**alto/alta** *altoh/altah*
short	**bajo/baja** *bahoh/bahah*
young	**joven** *hoben*
old	**viejo/vieja** *byayhoh/byayhah*
fat	**gordo/gorda** *gordoh/gordah*
thin	**delgado/delgada** *delgadoh/delgadah*
long/short hair	**el pelo largo/corto** *el peloh largoh/kortoh*
glasses	**las gafas** *las gafas*
beard	**la barba** *la barbah*

Cultural tip In Spain there is a difference between **la guardia civil** and **la policía**. **La policía** are the local police while **la guardia civil** operates in airports and patrols the national road system. The police uniforms are blue and those of the **guardia civil** are green.

5 Put into practice (2 minutes)

Practise these phrases. Then cover the text on the right and follow the instructions to make your reply in Spanish.

¿Cómo era?
komoh ehrah

What did he look like?

Say: Short and fat.

Bajo y gordo.
bahoh ee gordoh

¿Y el pelo?
ee el peloh

And his hair?

Say: Long with a beard.

Largo y con barba.
largoh ee kon barbah

Respuestas
Answers (Cover with flap)

REPASE Y REPITA
Review and repeat

1 To come

❶ **vienen**
byenen

❷ **viene**
byenay

❸ **venimos**
beneemos

❹ **venís**
benees

❺ **vengo**
bengoh

1 To come (3 minutes)

Put the correct form of **venir** (*to come*) in the gaps.

❶ Mis padres _____ a las cuatro.

❷ La asistenta _____ una vez a la semana.

❸ Nosotros _____ todos los martes.

❹ ¿ _____ vosotros con nosotros?

❺ Yo _____ en taxi.

2 Bank and post

❶ **los billetes**
los beeyetes

❷ **la postal**
lah postal

❸ **el paquete**
el paketay

❹ **el sobre**
el sobray

2 Bank and post (4 minutes)

Name these items.

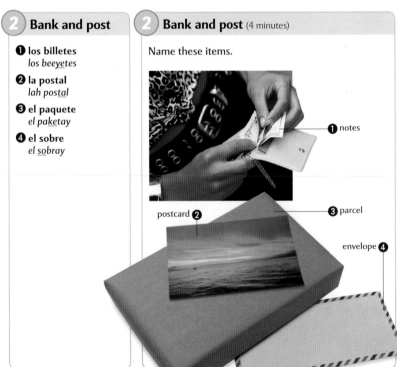

❶ notes

postcard ❷

❸ parcel

envelope ❹

3 Appearance (4 minutes)

What do these descriptions mean?

❶ Es un hombre alto y delgado.
❷ Ella tiene el pelo corto y gafas.
❸ Soy baja y tengo el pelo largo.
❹ Ella es vieja y gorda.
❺ Él tiene los ojos azules y barba.

3 Appearance

❶ He's a tall,
    thin man.
❷ She has short hair
    and glasses.
❸ I'm short and I
    have long hair.
❹ She's old and fat.
❺ He has blue eyes
    and a beard.

4 The pharmacy (4 minutes)

You are asking a pharmacist for advice. Join
in the conversation, replying in Spanish following
the English prompts.

   Buenos días, ¿qué desea?
❶ I have a cough.

   ¿Le duele el pecho?
❷ No, but I have a headache.

   Tiene estas pastillas.
❸ Do you have that as a syrup?

   Sí señor. Aquí tiene.
❹ Thank you. How much is that?

   Cuatro euros.
❺ Here you are. Goodbye.

4 The pharmacy

❶ **Tengo tos.**
   tengoh tos

❷ **No, pero me duele
   la cabeza.**
   *noh, peroh may dwelay
   lah kabethah*

❸ **¿Lo tiene en jarabe?**
   loh tyenay en harabay

❹ **Gracias. ¿Cuánto es?**
   grathyas. kwantoh es

❺ **Aquí tiene. Adiós.**
   ahkee tyenay. addy-os

① Warm up (1 minute)

What is the Spanish for "museum" and "art gallery"? (pp.48-9)

Say "I don't like the curtains". (pp.100-1)

Ask "Do you want...?" informally. (pp.22-3)

EL OCIO
Leisure time

The Spanish pride themselves on their lively nightlife and love for the arts, including theatre and film. It is not unusual for Spaniards to number politics or philosophy among their interests. Be prepared for these topics to be the subject of conversation in social situations.

② Words to remember (4 minutes)

Familiarize yourself with these words and test yourself using the cover flap to conceal the Spanish on the left.

el teatro *el te-ahtroh*	theatre
el cine *el theenay*	cinema
la discoteca *lah deeskotekah*	discotheque
el deporte *el deportay*	sport
el turismo *el tooreesmoh*	sightseeing
la política *la poleeteekah*	politics
la música *lah mooseekah*	music
el arte *el artay*	art

Me encanta el baile.
me enkantah el baeelay
I love dancing.

③ In conversation (4 minutes)

Hola. ¿Quieres jugar al tenis hoy?
o-lah. kyaires hoogar al tenis oy

Hi, do you want to play tennis today?

No, no me gusta el deporte.
noh, noh may goostah el deportay

No, I don't like sport.

Y entonces, ¿qué te gusta?
ee entonthes, kay tay goostah

So then, what do you like?

los video-juegos
los beedayoh-hwegos
video games

la bailadora
lah baeeladorah
dancer

el traje típico
el trahay teepeekoh
traditional costume

4 Useful phrases (4 minutes)

Learn these phrases and then test yourself using the cover flap.

What are your (formal/ informal) interests?	**¿Cuáles son sus/ tus intereses?** *kwales son soos/ toos intereses*
I like the theatre.	**Me gusta el teatro.** *may goostah el te-ahtroh*
I prefer the cinema.	**Yo prefiero el cine.** *yoh prefyairoh el theenay*
I'm interested in art.	**Me interesa el arte.** *may interesah el artay*
That bores me.	**Eso me aburre.** *ehsoh may aboorray*

5 Say it (2 minutes)

I'm interested in music.

I prefer sport.

I don't like video games.

Prefiero el turismo e ir de compras.
prefyairoh el tooreesmoh eh eer day kompras

I prefer sightseeing and shopping.

Eso a mí no me interesa.
ehsoh ah mee noh may interesah

That doesn't interest me.

No pasa nada. Me voy yo sola.
noh pasah nadah. may boy yoh solah

No problem. I'll go on my own.

EL DEPORTE Y LOS PASATIEMPOS
Sport and hobbies

1 Warm up (1 minute)

Ask "Do you (formal) want to play tennis?" (pp.118-19)

Say "I like the theatre" and "I prefer sightseeing". (pp.118-19)

Say "That doesn't interest me". (pp.118-19)

Hacer (*to do* or *to make*) and **jugar** (*to play*) are the verbs used most when talking about sport and pastimes. **Jugar** is followed by **al** when you are talking about playing a sport, as in **juego al baloncesto** (*I play basketball*).

2 Words to remember (5 minutes)

Familiarize yourself with these words and then test yourself.

el fútbol/rugby el <u>foot</u>bol/<u>roog</u>bee	football/rugby
el tenis/baloncesto el <u>ten</u>is/balon<u>thes</u>toh	tennis/ basketball
la natación lah natath<u>yon</u>	swimming
la vela lah <u>be</u>lah	sailing
la pesca lah <u>pes</u>kah	fishing
la pintura lah peen<u>too</u>rah	painting
el ciclismo el thee<u>klees</u>moh	cycling
el senderismo el sende<u>rees</u>moh	hiking

el búnker
 el <u>bun</u>ker <br> bunker

el jugador de golf
 el <u>hu</u>gador day golf <br> golfer

Juego al golf todos los días.
 <u>hwe</u>goh al golf todos los <u>dee</u>yas
 I play golf every day.

3 Useful phrases (2 minutes)

Learn these phrases and then test yourself.

Juego al fútbol. <u>hwe</u>goh al <u>foot</u>bol	I play football.
Juega al tenis. <u>hwe</u>gah al <u>ten</u>is	He plays tennis.
Ella pinta. eh-yah <u>peen</u>tah	She paints.

4 Hacer: to do or to make (4 minutes)

Hoy hace bueno.
oy ahthay bwenoh
It's nice (weather) today.

_____ **la banderola**
lah bandairolah
flag

_____ **el campo de golf**
el kampoh day golf
golf course

Hacer is a useful verb meaning *to do* or *to make*. It is commonly used to describe leisure pursuits. **Hace** is also used to describe the weather.

I do	**yo hago** *yoh ahgoh*
you do (informal/ formal singular)	**tú haces/usted hace** *too ahthes/oosted ahthay*
he/she does	**él/ella hace** *el/eh-yah ahthay*
we do	**nosotros(-as) hacemos** *nosotros(-as) ahthemos*
you do (informal plural)	**vosotros(-as) hacéis** *bosotros(-as) ahthays*
you do (formal plural)	**ustedes hacen** *oostedes ahthen*
they do	**ellos/ellas hacen** *eh-yos/eh-yas ahthen*
What do you like doing? (informal/formal singular)	**¿Qué te/le gusta hacer?** *kay tay/lay goostah ahthair?*
I go hiking.	**Yo hago senderismo.** *yoh ahgoh sendereesmoh*

5 Put into practice (3 minutes)

Join in this conversation following the English prompts.

¿Qué te gusta hacer?
kay tay goostah ahthair

What do you like doing?

Say: I like playing tennis.

Me gusta jugar al tenis.
may goostah hoogar al tenis

¿Juegas al fútbol también?
hwegas al footbol tambyen

Do you play football as well?

Say: No, I play rugby.

No, juego al rugby.
noh, hwegoh al roogbee

¿Cuándo juegas?
kwandoh hwegas

When do you play?

Say: I play every week.

Juego todas las semanas.
hwegoh todas las semanas

LA VIDA SOCIAL
Socializing

1 Warm up (1 minute)

Say "my husband" and "my wife". (pp.10-11)

Say the days of the week in Spanish. (pp.28-9)

Say "Sorry, I'm busy". (pp.32-3)

The dinner table is the centre of the Spanish social world. You can expect to do a lot of your socializing around the table, enjoying food and wine. In general it is best to use the more polite **usted** form to talk to older people and **tú** with the younger crowd.

la invitada
lah inbeetadah
guest

2 Useful phrases (3 minutes)

Practise these phrases and then test yourself.

Me gustaría invitarte a cenar. *may goostareeah inbeetartay ah thenar*	I'd like to invite you to dinner.
¿Estás libre el miércoles que viene? *estas leebray el myairkoles kay byenay*	Are you free next Wednesday?
Quizá otro día. *keethah ohtroh deeyah*	Perhaps another day.

Cultural tip When you visit someone's house for the first time, it is usual to bring flowers or wine. If you are invited again, having seen your host's house, you can bring something a little more personal.

3 In conversation (3 minutes)

¿Quieres venir a comer el martes?
kyaires beneer ah komer el martes

Would you like to come to lunch on Tuesday?

Lo siento, estoy ocupada.
loh syaintoh, estoy okoopadah

I'm sorry, I'm busy.

¿Qué tal el jueves?
kay tal el hwebes

What about Thursday?

la anfitriona
lah anfeetryonah
hostess

4 **Words to remember** (3 minutes)

Familiarize yourself with these words and test yourself using the flap.

party	**la fiesta** *lah fyaystah*
dinner party	**la cena** *lah thenah*
invitation	**la invitación** *lah inbeetathyon*
reception	**la recepción** *lah rrethepthyon*
cocktail party	**el coctel** *el koktel*

5 **Put into practice** (5 minutes)

Join this conversation, replying in Spanish.

¿Puede venir a una recepción esta noche?
pweday beneer ah oonah rrethepthyon estah nochay

Can you come to a reception tonight?

Say: Yes, I'd love to.

Sí, encantado/-a.
see, enkan-tadoh/-ah

Empieza a las ocho.
empyaythah ah las ochoh

It starts at eight o'clock.

Ask: What should I wear?

¿Qué me pongo?
kay may pongoh

Gracias por invitarnos.
grathyas por inbeetarnos
Thank you for inviting us.

Encantada.
enkan-tadah

I'd be delighted.

Ven con tu marido.
ben kon too mareedoh

Bring your husband.

Gracias, ¿a qué hora?
grathyas, ah kay orah

Thank you, at what time?

Respuestas
Answers (Cover with flap)

REPASE Y REPITA
Review and repeat

1 Animals

❶ **el pez**
el peth

❷ **el pájaro**
el paharoh

❸ **el conejo**
el konehoh

❹ **el gato**
el gatoh

❺ **el hámster**
el hamster

❻ **el perro**
el perroh

1 Animals (3 minutes)

Name the numbered animals in Spanish.

rabbit ❸

❶ fish

hamster ❺

❹ cat

2 I like...

❶ **Me gusta el fútbol.**
may goostah el footbol

❷ **No me gusta el golf.**
noh may goostah el golf

❸ **Me gusta pintar.**
may goostah peentar

❹ **No me gustan las flores.**
noh may goostan las flores

2 I like ... (4 minutes)

Say the following in Spanish:

❶ I like football.
❷ I don't like golf.
❸ I like painting.
❹ I don't like flowers.

❷ bird

❻ dog

3 Hacer (4 minutes)

Use the correct form of the verb **hacer** (*to do* or *to make*) in these sentences.

❶ Vosotros _____ senderismo.

❷ Ella _____ eso todos los días.

❸ ¿Qué _____ tú?

❹ Hoy no _____ frío.

❺ ¿Qué _____ ellos esta noche?

❻ Yo _____ natación.

3 Hacer

❶ **hacéis**
ahthays

❷ **hace**
ahthay

❸ **haces**
ahthes

❹ **hace**
ahthay

❺ **hacen**
ahthen

❻ **hago**
ahgoh

4 An invitation (4 minutes)

You are invited for dinner. Join in the conversation, replying in Spanish following the English prompts.

¿Quieres venir a comer el viernes?

❶ I'm sorry, I'm busy.

¿Qué tal el sábado?

❷ I'd be delighted.

Ven con los niños.

❸ Thank you. What time?

A las doce y media.

❹ That's good for me.

4 An invitation

❶ **Lo siento, estoy ocupado/-a.**
loh syentoh, estoy okoopadoh/-ah

❷ **Encantado/-a.**
enkantadoh/-ah

❸ **Gracias. ¿A qué hora?**
grathyas. ah kay orah

❹ **Me viene bien.**
may byenay byen

Reinforce and progress

Regular practice is the key to maintaining and advancing your language skills. In this section you will find a variety of suggestions for reinforcing and extending your knowledge of Spanish. Many involve returning to exercises in the book and using the dictionaries to extend their scope. Go back through the lessons in a different order, mix and match activities to make up your own 15-minute daily programme, or focus on topics that are of particular relevance to your current needs.

1 Warm up (1 minute)

Say "he is" and "they are". (pp.14-15)

Say "he is not" and "they are not". (pp.14-15)

What is Spanish for "the children"? (pp.10-11)

Keep warmed up
Re-visit the Warm Up boxes to remind yourself of key words and phrases. Make sure you work your way through all of them on a regular basis.

2 I'd like... (3 minutes)

Say "I'd like" the following:

❶ black coffee   churros ❷   ❸ sugar

white coffee ❹

Review and repeat again
Work through a Review and Repeat lesson as a way of reinforcing words and phrases presented in the course. Return to the main lesson for any topic on which you are no longer confident.

3 In conversation: taxi (2 minutes)

Carry on conversing
Re-read the In Conversation panels. Say both parts of the conversation, paying attention to the pronunciation. Where possible, try incorporating new words from the dictionary.

A la Plaza de España, por favor.
ah lah _plathah_ day espanyah, por _fabor_

Plaza de España, please.

Sí, de acuerdo, señor.
see, day ak_wairdo_, sen_yor_

Yes, certainly, sir.

¿Me puede dejar aquí, por favor?
may _pweday_ de_har_ ahkee, por _fabor_

Can you drop me here, please?

3 Useful phrases (5 minutes)

Practise these phrases and then test yourself using the cover flap.

The room is too cold/hot.	**Hace demasiado frío/calor en la habitación.** _ahthay daymasyahdoh freeoh/kalor en lah abeetathyon_
There are no towels.	**No hay toallas.** _noh ah-ee toh-ahyas_
I need some soap.	**Necesito jabón.** _netheseetoh habon_
The shower doesn't work.	**La ducha no funciona.** _lah doochah noh foonthyonah_

Practise phrases
Return to the Useful Phrases and Put into Practice exercises. Test yourself using the cover flap. When you are confident, devise your own versions of the phrases, using new words from the dictionary.

Match, repeat, and extend

Remind yourself of words related to specific topics by returning to the Match and Repeat and Words to Remember exercises. Test yourself using the cover flap. Discover new words in that area by referring to the dictionary and menu guide.

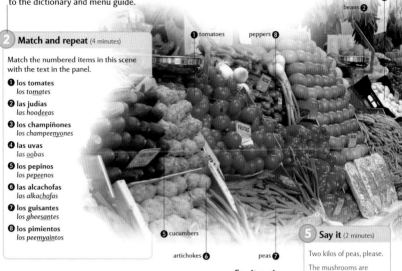

grapes **4**
mushrooms **3**
beans **2**
1 tomatoes
peppers **8**

2 Match and repeat (4 minutes)

Match the numbered items in this scene with the text in the panel.

1 los tomates
los to*mates*

2 las judías
las hoo*deeas*

3 los champiñones
los champee*nyones*

4 las uvas
las *oobas*

5 los pepinos
los pe*peenos*

6 las alcachofas
las alka*chofas*

7 los guisantes
los ghee*santes*

8 los pimientos
los peem*yaintos*

5 cucumbers
artichokes **6**
peas **7**

5 Say it (2 minutes)

Two kilos of peas, please.

The mushrooms are too expensive.

How much are the grapes?

Say it again
The Say It exercises are a useful instant reminder for each lesson. Practise these, using your own vocabulary variations from the dictionary or elsewhere in the lesson.

Using other resources

In addition to working with this book, try the following language extension ideas:

Visit a Spanish-speaking country and try out your new skills with native speakers. Find out if there is a Spanish community near you. There may be shops, cafés, restaurants, and clubs. Try to visit some of these and use your Spanish to order food and drink and strike up conversations. Most native speakers will be happy to speak Spanish to you.

Join a language class or club. There are usually evening and day classes available at different levels. Or you could start a club yourself if you have friends who are also interested in keeping up their Spanish.

Look at Spanish magazines and newspapers. The pictures will help you to understand the text. Advertisements are also a useful way of expanding your vocabulary.

Use the Internet, where you can find all kinds of websites for learning languages, some of which offer free online help and activities. You can also find Spanish websites for everything from renting a house to shampooing your pet. You can even access Spanish radio and TV stations online. Start by going to a Spanish search engine, such as ozu.es, and keying in a hobby or sport that interests you, or set yourself a challenge, such as finding a two-bedroom house for rent in Madrid.

MENU GUIDE

This guide lists the most common terms you may encounter on Spanish menus or when shopping for food. If you can't find an exact phrase, try looking up its component parts.

A

aceitunas *olives*
acelgas *spinach beet*
achicoria *chicory*
aguacate *avocado*
ahumados *smoked*
agua mineral *mineral water*
ajo *garlic*
al ajillo *with garlic*
a la parrilla *grilled*
a la plancha *grilled*
albaricoques *apricots*
albóndigas *meatballs*
alcachofas *artichokes*
alcaparras *capers*
al horno *baked*
allioli *garlic mayonnaise*
almejas *clams*
almejas a la marinera *clams stewed in wine and parsley*
almejas naturales *live clams*
almendras *almonds*
almíbar *syrup*
alubias *beans*
ancas de rana *frogs' legs*
anchoas *anchovies*
anguila *eel*
angulas *baby eels*
arenque *herring*
arroz a la cubana *rice with fried eggs and banana fritters*
arroz a la valenciana *rice with seafood*
arroz con leche *rice pudding*
asados *roast meat*
atún *tuna*
azúcar *sugar*

B

bacalao a la vizcaína *cod served with ham, peppers, and chillies*
bacalao al pil pil *cod served with chillies and garlic*
batido *milk shake*
bebidas *drinks*
berenjenas *aubergine*
besugo al horno *baked sea bream*
bistec de ternera *veal steak*
bonito *fish similar to tuna*
boquerones fritos *fried, fresh anchovies*
brazo gitano *swiss roll*
brocheta de riñones *kidney kebabs*
buñuelos *fried pastries*
butifarra *Catalan sausage*

C

cabrito asado *roast kid*
cacahuetes *peanuts*
cachelada *pork stew with eggs, tomato, and onion*
café *coffee*
café con leche *coffee with steamed milk*
calabacines *courgette*
calabaza *pumpkin*
calamares a la romana *squid rings in batter*
calamares en su tinta *squid cooked in their ink*
caldeirada *fish soup*
caldereta gallega *vegetable stew*
caldo de ... ... *soup*
caldo de gallina *chicken soup*
caldo de pescado *clear fish soup*
caldo gallego *vegetable soup*
caldo guanche *soup of potatoes, tomatoes, onions, and courgettes*
callos a la madrileña *tripe cooked with chillies*
camarones *baby prawns*
canela *cinnamon*
cangrejos *crabs*
caracoles *snails*
caramelos *sweets*
carnes *meats*
castañas *chestnuts*
cebolla *onion*
cebolletas *spring onions*
centollo *spider crab*
cerdo *pork*
cerezas *cherries*
cerveza *beer*
cesta de frutas *selection of fresh fruit*
champiñones *mushrooms*
chanquetes *fish (similar to whitebait)*

chipirones *baby squid*
chipirones en su tinta *squid cooked in their ink*
chocos *cuttlefish*
chorizo *spicy sausage*
chuleta de buey *beef chop*
chuleta de cerdo *pork chop*
chuleta de cerdo empanada *breaded pork chop*
chuleta de cordero *lamb chop*
chuleta de cordero empanada *breaded lamb chop*
chuleta de ternera *veal chop*
chuleta de ternera empanada *breaded veal chop*
chuletas de lomo ahumado *smoked pork chops*
chuletitas de cordero *small lamb chops*
chuletón *large chop*
chuletón de buey *large beef chop*
churros *deep-fried pastry strips*
cigalas *crayfish*
cigalas cocidas *boiled crayfish*
ciruelas *plums*
ciruelas pasas *prunes*
cochinillo asado *roast suckling pig*
cocido *meat, chickpea, and vegetable stew*
cocktail de bogavante *lobster cocktail*
cococas (de merluza) *hake stew*
cóctel de gambas *prawn cocktail*
cóctel de langostinos *jumbo prawn cocktail*
cóctel de mariscos *seafood cocktail*
codornices *quail*
codornices escabechadas *marinated quail*
codornices estofadas *braised quail*
col *cabbage*
coles de Bruselas *Brussels sprouts*
coliflor *cauliflower*
coñac *brandy*
conejo *rabbit*

conejo encebollado *rabbit with onions*
congrio *conger eel*
consomé con yema *consommé with egg yolk*
consomé de ave *fowl consommé*
contra de ternera con guisantes *veal stew with peas*
contrafilete de ternera *veal fillet*
copa *glass (of wine)*
copa de helado *ice cream, assorted flavours*
cordero asado *roast lamb*
cordero chilindrón *lamb stew with onion, tomato, peppers, and eggs*
costillas de cerdo *pork ribs*
crema catalana *crème brûlée*
cremada *dessert made with egg, sugar, and milk*
crema de... *cream of ... soup*
crema de legumbres *cream of vegetable soup*
crepe imperiale *crêpe suzette*
criadillas de tierra *truffles*
crocante *ice cream with chopped nuts*
croquetas *croquettes*
cuajada *curds*

D, E

dátiles *dates*
embutidos *sausages*
embutidos de la tierra *local sausages*
empanada gallega *fish pie*
empanada santiaguesa *fish pie*
empanadillas *small pies*
endivia *endive*
en escabeche *marinated*
ensalada *salad*
ensalada de arenque *fish salad*
ensalada ilustrada *mixed salad*
ensalada mixta *mixed salad*
ensalada simple *green salad*
ensaladilla rusa *Russian salad (potatoes, carrots, peas, and other vegetables in mayonnaise)*
entrecot a la parrilla *grilled entrecôte*
entremeses *hors d'oeuvres, starters*
escalope a la milanesa *breaded veal with cheese*
escalope a la parrilla *grilled veal*
escalope a la plancha *grilled veal*
escalope de lomo de cerdo *escalope of pork fillet*
escalope de ternera *veal escalope*

escalope empanado *breaded escalope*
escalopines al vino de Marsala *veal escalopes cooked in Marsala wine*
escalopines de ternera *veal escalopes*
espadín a la toledana *kebab*
espaguetis *spaghetti*
espárragos *asparagus*
espárragos trigueros *wild green asparagus*
espinacas *spinach*
espinazo de cerdo con patatas *stew of pork ribs with potatoes*
estofado *braised; stew*
estragón *tarragon*

F

fabada (asturiana) *bean stew with sausage*
faisán *pheasant*
faisán trufado *pheasant with truffles*
fiambres *cold meats*
fideos *thin pasta, noodles*
filete a la parrilla *grilled beef steak*
filete de cerdo *pork steak*
filete de ternera *veal steak*
flan *crème caramel*
frambuesas *raspberries*
fresas *strawberries*
fritos *fried*
fruta *fruit*

G

gallina en pepitoria *chicken stew with peppers*
gambas *prawns*
gambas cocidas *boiled prawns*
gambas en gabardina *prawns in batter*
gambas rebozadas *prawns in batter*
garbanzos *chickpeas*
garbanzos a la catalana *chickpeas with sausage, boiled eggs, and pine nuts*
gazpacho andaluz *cold tomato soup*
gelatina de ... ... *jelly*
gratén de ... ... *au gratin (baked in a cream and cheese sauce)*
granizada *crushed ice drink*
gratinada/o *au gratin*
grelo *turnip*
grillado *grilled*
guisantes *peas*
guisantes salteados *sautéed peas*

H

habas *broad beans*
habichuelas *white beans*
helado *ice cream*
helado de vainilla *vanilla ice cream*
helado de turrón *nougat ice cream*
hígado *liver*
hígado de ternera *calves' liver*
hígado estofado *braised liver*
higos con miel y nueces *figs with honey and nuts*
higos secos *dried figs*
horchata (de chufas) *cold drink made from chufa nuts*
huevo hilado *egg yolk garnish*
huevos *eggs*
huevos a la flamenca *fried eggs with ham, tomato, and vegetables*
huevos cocidos *hard-boiled eggs*
huevos con patatas fritas *fried eggs and chips*
huevos con picadillo *eggs with minced meat*
huevos duros *hard-boiled eggs*
huevos escalfados *poached eggs*
huevos pasados por agua *soft-boiled eggs*
huevos revueltos *scrambled eggs*

J

jamón *ham*
jamón con huevo hilado *ham with egg yolk garnish*
jamón serrano *cured ham*
jarra de vino *wine jug*
jerez *sherry*
jeta *pigs' cheeks*
judías verdes *green beans*
judías verdes a la española *bean stew*
judías verdes al natural *plain green beans*
jugo de ... ... *juice*

L

langosta *lobster*
langosta a la americana *lobster with brandy and garlic*
langosta a la catalana *lobster with mushrooms and ham in white sauce*
langosta fría con mayonesa *cold lobster with mayonnaise*
langostinos *king prawns*
langostinos dos salsas *king prawns cooked in two sauces*
laurel *bay leaves*

leche *milk*

leche frita *pudding made from milk and eggs*

leche merengada *cold milk with meringue*

lechuga *lettuce*

lengua de buey *ox tongue*

lengua de cordero *lambs' tongue*

lenguado a la romana *sole in batter*

lenguado meuniere *sole meunière (floured sole fried in butter)*

lentejas *lentils*

lentejas aliñadas *lentils in vinaigrette dressing*

licores *spirits, liqueurs*

liebre estofada *stewed hare*

lima *lime*

limón *lemon*

lombarda *red cabbage*

lomo curado *pork loin sausage*

lonchas de jamón *sliced, cured ham*

longaniza *cooked Spanish sausage*

lubina *sea bass*

lubina a la marinera *sea bass in a parsley sauce*

M

macedonia de fruta *fruit salad*

mahonesa *or* mayonesa *mayonnaise*

Málaga *a sweet wine*

mandarinas *tangerines*

manitas de cordero *lamb shank*

manos de cerdo *pigs' feet*

manos de cerdo a la parrilla *grilled pigs' feet*

mantecadas *small sponge cakes*

mantequilla *butter*

manzanas *apples*

mariscada *cold mixed shellfish*

mariscos del día *fresh shellfish*

mariscos del tiempo *seasonal shellfish*

medallones *steaks*

media de agua *half bottle of mineral water*

mejillones *mussels*

mejillones a la marinera *mussels in a wine sauce*

melocotón *peach*

melón *melon*

menestra de legumbres *vegetable stew*

menú de la casa *set menu*

menú del día *set menu*

merluza *hake*

merluza a la cazuela *stewed hake*

merluza al ajo arriero *hake with garlic and chillies*

merluza a la riojana *hake with chillies*

merluza a la romana *hake steaks in batter*

merluza a la vasca *hake in a garlic sauce*

merluza en salsa *hake in sauce*

merluza en salsa verde *hake in a green (parsley and wine) sauce*

merluza fría *cold hake*

merluza frita *fried hake*

mermelada *jam*

mero *grouper (fish)*

mero en salsa verde *grouper in green (garlic and parsley) sauce*

mollejas de ternera fritas *fried sweetbreads*

morcilla *blood sausage*

morcilla de carnero *mutton blood sausage*

morros de cerdo *pigs' cheeks*

morros de vaca *cows' cheeks*

mortadela *salami-type sausage*

morteruelo *kind of pâté*

N, O

nabo *turnip*

naranjas *oranges*

nata *cream*

natillas *cold custard*

níscalos *wild mushrooms*

nueces *walnuts*

orejas de cerdo *pigs' ears*

P

paella *fried rice with seafood and/or meat*

paella castellana *meat paella*

paella valenciana *shellfish, rabbit, and chicken paella*

paleta de cordero lechal *shoulder of lamb*

pan *bread*

panache de verduras *vegetable stew*

panceta *bacon*

parrillada de caza *mixed grilled game*

parrillada de mariscos *mixed grilled shellfish*

pasas *raisins*

pastel de ternera *veal pie*

pasteles *cakes*

patatas a la pescadora *potatoes with fish*

patatas asadas *baked potatoes*

patatas bravas *potatoes in spicy tomato sauce*

patatas fritas *chips*

patitos rellenos *stuffed duckling*

pato a la naranja *duck in orange sauce*

pavo *turkey*

pavo trufado *turkey stuffed with truffles*

pecho de ternera *breast of veal*

pechuga de pollo *breast of chicken*

pepinillos *gherkins*

pepino *cucumber*

peras *pears*

percebes *edible barnacle*

perdices a la campesina *partridges with vegetables*

perdices a la manchega *partridges in red wine, garlic, herbs, and pepper*

perdices escabechadas *marinated partridges*

perejil *parsley*

perritos calientes *hot dogs*

pescaditos fritos *fried fish*

pestiños *sugared pastries flavoured with aniseed*

pez espada *swordfish*

picadillo de ternera *minced veal*

pimienta *black pepper*

pimientos *peppers*

pimientos a la riojana *baked red peppers fried in oil and garlic*

pimientos morrones *a type of bell pepper*

pimientos verdes *green peppers*

piña al gratín *pineapple au gratin*

piña fresca *fresh pineapple*

pinchitos/pinchos *kebabs, snacks served in bars*

pinchos morunos *pork kebabs*

piñones *pine nuts*

pisto *ratatouille*

pisto manchego *vegetable marrow with onion and tomato*

plátanos *bananas*

plátanos flameados *flambéed bananas*

pollo *chicken*

pollo a la riojana *chicken with peppers and chillies*

pollo al ajillo *fried chicken with garlic*

pollo asado *roast chicken*

pollo braseado *braised chicken*

pollo en cacerola *chicken casserole*

pollo en pepitoria *chicken in wine with saffron, garlic, and almonds*

pollos tomateros con zanahorias *young chicken with carrots*

pomelo *grapefruit*

potaje castellano *thick broth*

potaje de ... ... *stew*

puchero canario *casserole of meat, chickpeas, and corn*
pulpitos con cebolla *baby octopus with onions*
pulpo *octopus*
puré de patatas *mashed potatoes, potato purée*
purrusalda *cod with leeks and potatoes*

Q

queso con membrillo *cheese with quince jelly*
queso de bola *Dutch cheese*
queso de Burgos *soft white cheese*
queso del país *local cheese*
queso de oveja *sheep's cheese*
queso gallego *a creamy cheese*
queso manchego *a hard, strong cheese*
quisquillas *shrimps*

R

rábanos *radishes*
ragout de ternera *veal ragoût*
rape a la americana *monkfish with brandy and herbs*
rape a la cazuela *stewed monkfish*
raya *skate*
rebozado *in batter*
redondo al horno *roast fillet of beef*
rellenos *stuffed*
remolacha *beetroot*
repollo *cabbage*
repostería de la casa *cakes baked on the premises*
requesón *cream cheese, cottage cheese*
revuelto de ... *scrambled eggs with ...*
revuelto de ajos tiernos *scrambled eggs with spring garlic*
revuelto de trigueros *scrambled eggs with asparagus*
revuelto mixto *scrambled eggs with mixed vegetables*
riñones *kidneys*
rodaballo *turbot (fish)*
romero *rosemary*
ron *rum*
roscas *sweet pastries*

S

sal *salt*
salchichas *sausages*
salchichas de Frankfurt *hot dog sausages*

salchichón *sausage similar to salami*
salmón ahumado *smoked salmon*
salmonetes *red mullet*
salmonetes en papillote *red mullet cooked in foil*
salmón frío *cold salmon*
salmorejo *sauce of bread, tomatoes, oil, vinegar, green pepper, and garlic*
salpicón de mariscos *shellfish in vinaigrette*
salsa bechamel *white sauce*
salsa holandesa *hollandaise sauce*
sandía *watermelon*
sardinas a la brasa *barbecued sardines*
seco *dry*
semidulce *medium-sweet*
sesos *brains*
sesos a la romana *fried brains in batter*
sesos rebozados *brains in batter*
setas *mushrooms*
sidra *cider*
sobreasada *sausage with cayenne pepper*
solomillo *fillet steak*
solomillo con patatas *fillet steak with chips*
solomillo de ternera *fillet of veal*
solomillo de vaca *fillet of beef*
solomillo frío *cold roast beef*
sopa *soup*
sopa castellana *vegetable soup*
sopa de almendras *almond soup*
sopa de cola de buey *oxtail soup*
sopa de gallina *chicken soup*
sopa del día *soup of the day*
sopa de legumbres *vegetable soup*
sopa de marisco *fish and shellfish soup*
sopa de rabo de buey *oxtail soup*
sopa mallorquina *soup of tomato, meat, and eggs*
sopa sevillana *fish and mayonnaise soup*
soufflé de fresones *strawberry soufflé*

T

tallarines *noodles*
tallarines a la italiana *tagliatelle*
tarta *cake*
tarta de la casa *cake baked on the premises*

tarta de manzana *apple tart*
tencas *tench*
ternera asada *roast veal*
tocinillos del cielo *a very sweet crème caramel*
tomates *tomatoes*
tomillo *thyme*
torrijas *sweet pastries*
tortilla a la paisana *vegetable omelette*
tortilla a su gusto *omelette made to the customer's wishes*
tortilla de escabeche *fish omelette*
tortilla española *Spanish omelette with potato, onion, and garlic*
tortilla sacromonte *vegetable, brains, and sausage omelette*
tortillas variadas *assorted omelettes*
tournedó *fillet steak*
trucha *trout*
trucha ahumada *smoked trout*
trucha escabechada *marinated trout*
truchas a la marinera *trout in wine sauce*
truchas molinera *trout meunière (floured trout fried in butter)*
trufas *truffles*
turrón *nougat*

U, V

uvas *grapes*
verduras *vegetables*
vieiras *scallops*
vino de mesa/blanco / rosado/tinto *table/ white/rosé/ red wine*

Z

zanahorias a la crema *creamed carrots*
zarzuela de mariscos *seafood stew*
zarzuela de pescados y mariscos *fish and shellfish stew*
zumo de ... ... *juice*

DICTIONARY
English to Spanish

The gender of a Spanish noun is indicated by the word for *the*: **el** and **la** (masculine and feminine singular) or their plural forms **los** (masculine) and **las** (feminine). Spanish adjectives (adj) vary according to the gender and number of the word they describe, and the masculine form is shown here. In general, adjectives that end in **-o** adopt an **-a** ending in the feminine form, and those that end in **-e** usually stay the same. For the plural form, an **-s** is added.

A

a **un/una**
able: to be able **poder**
about: about sixteen **alrededor de dieciséis**
accelerator **el acelerador**
accident **el accidente**
accommodation **el alojamiento**
accountant **el/la contable**
ache **el dolor**
adaptor **el adaptador**
address **la dirección**
adhesive **el pegamento**
admission charge **el precio de entrada**
after ... **después de ...**
aftershave **el after-shave**
again **otra vez**
against **contra**
agenda **el orden del día**
agency **la agencia**
AIDS **el Sida**
air **el aire**
air conditioning **el aire acondicionado**
aircraft **el avión**
airline **la compañía aérea**
air mail **por avión**
air mattress **la colchoneta**
airport **el aeropuerto**
airport bus **el autobús del aeropuerto**
aisle **el pasillo**
alarm clock **el despertador**
alcohol **el alcohol**
Algeria **Argelia**
all **todo;** *all the streets* **todas las calles;** *that's all* **eso es todo**
allergic **alérgico**
almost **casi**
alone **solo**
already **ya**
always **siempre**
am: I am **soy/estoy**

ambulance **la ambulancia**
America **América**
American **el americano/ la americana**
and **y;** (after 'i' or 'h') **e**
angle-poise lamp **el flexo**
ankle **el tobillo**
another **otro**
answering machine **el contestador automático**
antifreeze **el anticongelante**
antique shop **el anticuario**
antiseptic **el antiséptico**
apartment **el apartamento, el piso**
aperitif **el aperitivo**
appetite **el apetito**
apple **la manzana**
application form **el impreso de solicitud**
appointment (business) **la cita;** (at hairdresser's) **hora**
apricot **el albaricoque**
April **abril**
are: you are (informal singular) **eres/estás;** (formal singular) **es/está;** (informal plural) **sois/ estáis;** (formal plural) **son/están;** *we are* **somos/ estamos;** *they are* **son/están**
arm **el brazo**
arrive **llegar**
art **el arte**
art gallery **la galería de arte**
artichoke **la alcachofa**
artist **el/la artista**
as: as soon as possible **lo antes posible**
ashtray **el cenicero**
asleep: he's asleep **está dormido**
aspirin **la aspirina**
asthmatic **asmático**

at: at the post office **en Correos;** *at night* **por la noche;** *at 3 o'clock* **a las tres**
Atlantic Ocean **el Océano Atlántico**
ATM **el cajero automático**
attic **el ático**
attractive (person) **guapo;** (object) **bonito;** (offer) **atractivo**
aubergines **las berenjenas**
August **agosto**
aunt **la tía**
Australia **Australia**
Australian **el australiano/ la australiana;** (adj) **australiano**
automatic **automático**
available **disponible**
away: is it far away? **¿está lejos?;** *go away!* **¡váyase!**
awful **horrible**
axe **el hacha**
axle **el eje**

B

baby **el niño pequeño, el bebé**
baby wipes **las toallitas para bebé**
back (not front) **la parte de atrás;** (body) **la espalda**
backpack **la mochila**
bacon **el bacon;** *bacon and eggs* **los huevos fritos con bacon**
bad **malo**
bag **la bolsa**
bait **el cebo**
bake **cocer al horno**
bakery **la panadería**
balcony **el balcón**
Balearic Islands **las (Islas) Baleares**
ball (football) **el balon;** (tennis etc) **la pelota**

ballpoint pen **el bolígrafo**
banana **el plátano**
band (musicians) **la banda**
bandage **la venda**
bank **el banco**
bank card **la tarjeta de banco**
banknote **el billete de banco**
bar (drinks) **el bar**
barbecue **la barbacoa**
barber **la peluquería**
   de caballeros
bargain **la ganga**
basement **el sótano**
basin (sink) **el lavabo**
basket **el cesto**
basketball **el baloncesto**
bath **el baño;** *to have*
   a bath **darse un baño**
bathing suit **el bañador,**
   el traje de baño
bathroom **el cuarto de baño**
battery (car) **la batería;**
   (torch etc) **la pila**
Bay of Biscay **el Golfo**
   de Vizcaya
be **ser/estar**
beach **la playa**
beach ball **el balón de playa**
beans **las judías**
beard **la barba**
beautiful (object) **precioso;**
   (person) **guapo**
beauty products **los**
   productos de belleza
because **porque**
bed **la cama**
bed linen **la ropa de cama**
bedroom **el dormitorio**
bedside lamp
   la lamparilla de noche
bedside table **la mesilla**
   de noche
bedspread **la colcha**
beef **la carne de vaca**
beer **la cerveza**
before ... **antes de** ...
beginner **el/la principiante**
behind ... **detrás de** ...
beige **beige**
bell (church) **la campana;**
   (door) **el timbre**
below **debajo de**
belt **el cinturón**
beside **al lado de**
best (el) **mejor**
better **mejor**
between **entre**
bicycle **la bicicleta**
big **grande**
bill **la cuenta**
bin **el contendor de basura**

bin liner **la bolsa de basura**
bird **el pájaro**
birthday **el cumpleaños;**
   happy birthday! **¡felicidades!**
birthday present **el regalo**
   de cumpleaños
biscuit **la galleta**
bite (by dog) **la mordedura;**
   (by insect) **la picadura;**
   (verb: by dog) **morder;**
   (by insect) **picar**
black **negro**
blackberries **las moras**
blackcurrants **las grosellas**
   negras
blanket **la manta**
bleach **la lejía;** (verb: hair)
   teñir
blind (cannot see) **ciego**
blinds **las persianas**
blister **la ampolla**
blizzard **la ventisca**
blond(e) (adj) **rubio**
blood **la sangre**
blood test **el análisis**
   de sangre
blouse **la blusa**
blue **azul**
boarding pass **la tarjeta**
   de embarque
boat **el barco;** (small)
   la barca
body **el cuerpo**
boil (verb: water) **hervir;**
   (egg etc) **cocer**
boiled **hervido**
bolt (on door) **el cerrojo;**
   (verb) **echar el cerrojo**
bone **el hueso**
bonnet (car) **el capó**
book **el libro;** (verb) **reservar**
bookshop **la librería**
boot (footwear) **la bota;**
   (car) **el maletero**
border **el borde;** (between
   countries) **la frontera**
boring **aburrido**
born: I was born in ...
   nací en ...
both: both of them **los dos;**
   both of us **los dos;** *both* ...
   and ... **tanto** ... **como** ...
bottle **la botella**
bottle opener **el abrebotellas**
bottom **el fondo;** (part of
   body) **el trasero**
bowl **el cuenco**
box **la caja**
box office **la taquilla**
boy **el chico**
boyfriend **el novio**

bra **el sostén**
bracelet **la pulsera**
braces (clothing) **los tirantes**
brake **el freno;** (verb) **frenar**
branch (of company)
   la oficina
brandy **el coñac**
bread **el pan**
breakdown (car) **la avería;**
   (nervous) **la crisis nerviosa;**
   I've had a breakdown (car)
   he tenido una avería
breakfast **el desayuno**
breathe **respirar**
bridge **el puente;** (game)
   el bridge
briefcase **la cartera**
British **británico**
brochure **el folleto**
broken **roto**
brooch **el broche**
brother **el hermano**
brown **marrón;** (hair)
   castaño; (skin) **moreno**
bruise **el cardenal**
brush (paint) **la brocha;**
   (cleaning) **el cepillo;**
   (hair) **el cepillo del pelo;**
   (verb: hair) **cepillar el pelo**
budget **el presupuesto**
bucket **el cubo**
builder **el albañil**
building **el edificio**
bull **el toro**
bullfight **la corrida de toros**
bullfighter **el torero**
bullring **la plaza de toros**
bumper **el parachoques**
burglar **el ladrón**
burn **la quemadura;**
   (verb) **quemar**
bus **el autobús**
business **el negocio;**
   it's none of your business
   no es asunto suyo
business card **la tarjeta**
   de vista
bus station **la estación**
   de autobuses
busy (bar) **concurrido;**
   (engaged) **ocupado**
but **pero**
butcher's **la carnicería**
butter **la mantequilla**
button **el botón**
buy **comprar**
by: by the window **junto a la**
   ventana; *by Friday* **para el**
   viernes; *by myself* **yo solo;**
   written by **escrito por**

C

cabbage **la col**
cable car **el teleférico**
cable TV **la television**
   por cable
café **el café**
cage **la jaula**
cake (small) **el pastel;**
   (large) **la tarta;**
   sponge cake **el bizcocho**
cake shop **la pastelería**
calculator **la calculadora**
call: what's it called?
   ¿cómo se llama?
camcorder **la videocámara**
camera **la máquina de
   fotos, la cámara de fotos**
camper van **la autocaravana**
campfire **la hoguera**
camping gas **el camping-gas**
campsite **el camping**
camshaft **el árbol de levas**
can (tin) **la lata;** (verb: to be
   able) **poder;** can you ...?
   ¿puede ...?; I can't ...
   no puedo ...
Canada **Canadá**
Canadian **canadiense**
canal **el canal**
Canaries **las (Islas) Canarias**
candle **la vela**
can opener **el abrelatas**
cap (bottle) **el tapón;** (hat)
   la gorra
car **el coche**
caravan **la roulotte**
carburetor **el carburador**
card **la tarjeta**
cardigan **la rebeca**
careful **prudente;**
   be careful! **¡cuidado!**
caretaker **el portero,
   el encargado**
car park **el aparcamiento**
carpenter **el carpintero**
carpet **la alfombra**
carriage (train) **el vagón**
carrot **la zanahoria**
car seat (for baby/child)
   el asiento infantil
case (suitcase) **la maleta**
cash **el dinero; cobrar**
   (verb); to pay cash **pagar
   al contado**
cashier **el cajero**
cashpoint **el cajero
   automático**
cassette **la cassette, la cinta**
cassette player **el cassette**
castanets **las castañuelas**

Castile **Castilla**
Castilian **castellano**
castle **el castillo**
cat **el gato**
Catalonia **Cataluña**
catch (bus etc) **coger**
cathedral **la catedral**
Catholic (adj) **católico**
cauliflower **la coliflor**
cave **la cueva**
ceiling **el techo**
cellar **la bodega**
cemetery **el cementerio**
central heating
   la calefacción central
centre **el centro**
certificate **el certificado**
chair **la silla**
change (money) **el cambio;**
   (verb: money) **cambiar;**
   (clothes) **cambiarse;**
   (trains etc) **hacer
   transbordo**
charger **el cargador**
check-in (desk)
   **la (el mostrador de)
   facturación**
check in (verb) **facturar**
check-out (supermarket)
   la caja
cheers! (toast) **¡salud!**
cheese **el queso**
chemist **la farmacia**
cheque **el cheque**
chequebook **el talonario
   de cheques**
cherry **la cereza**
chess **el ajedrez**
chest (part of body) **el pecho;**
   (furniture) **el arcón**
chest of drawers **la cómoda**
chewing gum **el chicle**
chicken **el pollo**
child **el niño/la niña**
children **los niños**
children's ward
   la sala de pediatría
chimney **la chimenea**
china **la porcelana**
chips **las patatas fritas**
chocolate **el chocolate;**
   box of chocolates **la caja de
   bombones;** chocolate bar
   la tableta de chocolate
chop **la chuleta;**
   (verb: cut) **cortar**
Christmas **la navidad**
church **la iglesia**
cigar **el puro**
cigarette **el cigarrillo**
cinema **el cine**

city **la ciudad**
city centre **el centro**
class **la clase**
classical music
   la música clásica
clean (adj) **limpio**
cleaner **la asistenta**
clear (obvious) **evidente;**
   (water) **claro**
clever **listo**
client **el cliente**
clock **el reloj**
close (near) **cerca;** (stuffy)
   sofocante; (verb) **cerrar**
closed **cerrado**
clothes **la ropa**
clubs (cards) **tréboles**
coat **el abrigo**
coat hanger **la percha**
cockroach **la cucaracha**
cocktail party **el coctel**
coffee **el café**
coin **la moneda**
cold (illness) **el resfriado;**
   (adj) **frío;** I have a cold
   tengo un resfriado;
   I'm cold **tengo frío**
collar **el cuello;** (of animal)
   el collar
collection (stamps etc)
   la colección; (postal)
   la recogida
colour **el color**
colour film **la película en color**
comb **el peine;** (verb) **peinar**
come **venir;** I come from ...
   soy de ...; we came
   last week **llegamos
   la semana pasada;**
   come here! **¡venga aquí!**
come back **volver**
compact disc
   el disco compacto
compartment
   el compartimento
complicated **complicado**
computer **el ordenador**
computer games
   los vídeo-juegos
concert **el concierto**
conditioner (hair)
   el acondicionador
condom **el condón**
conductor (bus) **el cobrador;**
   (orchestra) **el director**
conference **la conferencia**
conference room **la sala de
   conferencias**
congratulations!
   ¡enhorabuena!
consulate **el consulado**

contact lenses
las lentes de contacto
contraceptive el anticonceptivo
contract el contrato
cook el cocinero/la
cocinera; (verb) guisar
cooker la cocina
cooking utensils los utensilios
de cocina
cool fresco
cork el corcho
corkscrew el sacacorchos
corner (of street) la esquina;
(of room) el rincón
corridor el pasillo
cosmetics los cosméticos
cost (verb) costar; what does
it cost? ¿cuánto cuesta?
cot la cuna
cotton el algodón
cotton wool el algodón
cough la tos; (verb) toser
cough drops las pastillas
para la garganta
country (state) el país
countryside el campo
cousin el primo/la prima
crab el cangrejo
cramp el calambre
crayfish las cigalas
cream (dairy) la nata;
(lotion) la crema
credit card la tarjeta
de crédito
crib el capazo
crisps las patatas fritas
crowded lleno
cruise el crucero
crutches las muletas
cry (weep) llorar;
(shout) gritar
cucumber el pepino
cuff links los gemelos
cup la taza
cupboard el armario
curlers los rulos
curls los rizos
curry el curry
curtain la cortina
cushion el cojín
customs la aduana
cut la cortadura; (verb) cortar
cycling el ciclismo

D

dad papá
dairy products
los productos lácteos
damp húmedo
dance el baile; (verb) bailar

dangerous peligroso
dark oscuro; dark blue
azul oscuro
daughter la hija
day el día
dead muerto
deaf sordo
dear (person) querido
December diciembre
deck of cards la baraja
decorator el pintor
deep profundo
delayed retrasado
deliberately a propósito
delicatessen la charcutería
delivery la entrega
dentist el/la dentista
dentures la dentadura postiza
deny negar
deodorant el desodorante
department el departemento
department store
los grandes almacenes
departure la salida
departures las salidas
deposit la señal
designer el diseñador/
la diseñadora
desk la mesa de escritorio
dessert el postre
develop (film) revelar
diabetic diabético
diamonds (jewels) los
diamantes; (cards)
los diamantes
diarrhoea la diarrea
diary la agenda
dictionary el
diccionario
die morir
diesel (oil) fuel-oil;
(adj: engine) diesel
different diferente; that's
different! ¡eso es distinto!;
I'd like a different one
quisiera otro distinto
difficult difícil
dining room el comedor
dinner la cena
dinner party la cena
dirty sucio
disabled minusválido
discount el descuento
dish cloth el paño de cocina
dishwasher el lavavajillas
disposable nappies los
pañales desechables
divorced divorciado
do hacer
dock el muelle
doctor el médico/la médica

document el documento
dog el perro
doll la muñeca
dollar el dólar
door la puerta
double room
la habitación doble
doughnut el dónut
down hacia abajo
drawing pin la chincheta
dress el vestido
drink la bebida; (verb)
beber; would you like
something to drink?
¿quiere beber algo?
drinking water agua potable
drive (verb) conducir
driver el conductor
driving licence el carnet
de conducir
drops las gotas
drunk borracho
dry seco; (sherry) fino
dry cleaner la tintorería
during durante
dustbin el cubo de la basura
duster el trapo del polvo
duty-free libre de impuestos;
duty-free shop el duty-free
duvet el edredón

E

each (every) cada;
20 euros each
veinte euros cada uno
ear (inner) el oído; (outer)
la oreja; ears las orejas
early temprano
earrings los pendientes
east este; the East el Este
easy fácil
eat comer
egg el huevo
eight ocho
eighteen dieciocho
eighty ochenta
either: either of them
cualquiera de ellos; either
... or ... o bien ... o ...
elastic elástico
elbow el codo
electric eléctrico
electrician el/la electricista
electricity la electricidad
eleven once
else: something else algo más;
someone else alguien más;
somewhere else en otro sitio
email el email, el correo
electrónico

email address la dirección de email
embarrassing embarazoso
embassy la embajada
embroidery el bordado
emergency la emergencia
emergency brake (train) el freno de emergencia
emergency department el servicio de urgencias
emergency exit la salida de emergencia
employee el empleado
empty vacío
end el final
engaged (marriage) prometido/prometida; (telephone) ocupado
engine (motor) el motor
engineering la ingeniería
England Inglaterra
English inglés
Englishman el inglés
Englishwoman la inglesa
enlargement la ampliación
enough bastante
entertainment las diversiones
entrance la entrada
envelope el sobre
epileptic epiléptico
eraser la goma de borrar
escalator la escalera mecánica
especially sobre todo
espresso el café solo
estimate el presupuesto
evening la tarde
every cada; *every day* todos los días
everyone todos
everything todo
everywhere por todas partes
example el ejemplo; *for example* por ejemplo
excellent excelente
excess baggage exceso de equipaje
exchange (verb) cambiar
exchange rate el cambio
excursion la excursión
excuse me! (to get attention) ¡oiga, por favor!; (when sneezing etc) ¡perdón!; *excuse me, please* (to get past) ¿me hace el favor?
executive el ejecutivo
exhaust el tubo de escape
exhibition la exposición

exit la salida
expensive caro
extension cord el cable alargador
eye el ojo
eyebrow la ceja

F

face la cara
faint (unclear) tenue; (verb) desmayarse; *I feel faint* estoy mareado
fair la feria; *it's not fair* no hay derecho
false teeth la dentadura postiza
family la familia
fan (enthusiast) el fan; (football) el hincha; (ventilator) el ventilador; (handheld) el abanico
fantastic fantástico
far lejos; *how far is it to ...?* ¿qué distancia hay a ...?
fare el billete, la tarifa
farm la granja
farmer el granjero
fashion la moda
fast rápido
fat (adj) gordo; (on meat) la grasa
father el padre
fax el fax; (verb) enviar por fax
February febrero
feel (touch) tocar; *I feel hot* tengo calor; *I feel like ...* me apetece ...; *I don't feel well* no me encuentro bien
felt-tip pen el rotulador
fence la cerca
ferry el ferry
fiancé el prometido
fiancée la prometida
field (of grass etc) el campo; (of study) la especialidad
fifteen quinze
fifty cincuenta
fig el higo
figures los números
filling (in tooth) el empaste; (in sandwich, cake) el relleno
film la película
filter el filtro
filter papers los papeles de filtro

finger el dedo
fire el fuego; (blaze) el incendio
fire extinguisher el extintor
fireplace la chimenea
fireworks los fuegos artificiales
first primero; *first aid* primeros auxilios
first class de primera
first floor el primer piso
first name el nombre de pila
fish el pez; (food) el pescado
fishing la pesca; *to go fishing* ir a pescar
fishmonger's la pescadería
five cinco
fizzy water el agua con gas
flag la bandera
flash (camera) el flash
flat (level) plano
flat tyre la rueda pinchada
flavour el sabor
flea la pulga
flea spray el spray antipulgas
flight el vuelo
floor el suelo; (storey) el piso
flour la harina
flower la flor
flowerbed el parterre
flute la flauta
fly (insect) la mosca; (verb: of plane, insect) volar; (of person) viajar en avión
flyover el paso elevado
fog la niebla
folk music la música folklórica
food la comida
food poisoning la intoxicación alimenticia
foot el pie
football el fútbol; (ball) el balón
for: for me para mí; *what for?* ¿para qué?; *for a week* (para) una semana
foreigner el extranjero/la extranjera
forest el bosque; (tropical) la selva
forget olvidar
fork el tenedor; (garden) la horca
forty cuarenta
fountain la fuente
fountain pen la (pluma) estilográfica
four cuatro
fourteen catorce
fourth cuarto

France **Francia**
free (not engaged) **libre;**
(no charge) **gratis**
freezer **el congelador**
French **francés**
Friday **viernes**
fridge **el frigorífico**
fried **frito**
friend **el amigo/la amiga**
friendly **simpático**
fringe (hair) **el flequillo**
front: in front of ...
delante de ...
frost **la escarcha**
frozen foods **los congelados**
fruit **la fruta**
fruit juice **el zumo de frutas**
fry **freír**
frying pan **la sartén**
full **lleno;** *I'm full*
(up) **estoy lleno**
full board **pensión completa**
funny **divertido;** (odd) **raro**
furniture **los muebles**

G

garage (for parking) **el garage;**
(for repairs) **el taller**
garden **el jardín**
garden centre **el vivero**
garlic **el ajo**
gas-permeable lenses
las lentes de contacto
semi-rígidas
gate **la puerta, la verja;**
(at airport) **la puerta**
de embarque
gay (homosexual) **gay**
gearbox **la caja de cambios**
gear stick **la palanca**
de velocidades
gel (hair) **el gel**
German **alemán**
Germany **Alemania**
get (fetch) **traer;** *have you*
got ...? **¿tiene ...?;** *to get*
the train **coger el tren**
get back: we get back tomorrow
nos volvemos mañana;
to get something back
recobrar algo
get in (of train etc) **subirse;**
(of person) **llegar**
get off (bus etc) **bajarse**
get on (bus etc) **subirse**
get out **bajarse;**
(bring out) **sacar**
get up (rise) **levantarse**
Gibraltar **Gibraltar**
gift **el regalo**

gin **la ginebra**
ginger (spice) **el jengibre**
girl **la chica**
girlfriend **la novia**
give **dar**
glad **alegre**
glass (material) **el cristal;**
(for drinking) **el vaso,**
la copa
glasses **las gafas**
gloss prints **las copias**
con brillo
gloves **los guantes**
glue **el pegamento**
go **ir**
gold **el oro**
good **bueno;** *good!* **¡bien!**
good afternoon **buenas tardes**
goodbye **adiós**
good evening **buenas noches**
good morning **buenos días**
government **el gobierno**
granddaughter **la nieta**
grandfather **el abuelo**
grandmother **la abuela**
grandparents **los abuelos**
grandson **el nieto**
grapes **las uvas**
grass **la hierba**
Great Britain **Gran Bretaña**
green **verde**
greengrocer's **la verdulería**
grey **gris**
grill **la parrilla**
grilled **a la plancha**
grocer's **el ultramarinos,**
la tienda de comestibles
ground floor **la planta baja**
groundsheet **la lona**
impermeable,
el suelo aislante
guarantee **la garantía;**
(verb) **garantizar**
guest **la invitada**
guide **el/la guía**
guide book **la guía turística**
guided tour **la visita con guía**
guitar **la guitarra**
gun (rifle) **la escopeta;**
(pistol) **la pistola**

H

hair **el pelo**
haircut **el corte de pelo**
hairdresser's **la peluquería**
hairdryer **el secador** (de pelo)
hairspray **la laca**
half **medio;**
half an hour **media hora**
half board **media pensión**

ham **el jamón**
hamburger **la hamburguesa**
hammer **el martillo**
hamster **el hámster**
hand **la mano**
handbag **el bolso**
handbrake **el freno de mano**
handle (door) **el picaporte**
hand luggage
el equipaje de mano
handshake
el apretón de manos
handsome **guapo**
hangover **la resaca**
happy **contento, feliz**
harbour **el puerto**
hard **duro;** (difficult) **difícil**
hardware store **la ferretería**
hat **el sombrero;**
(woollen) **el gorro**
have **tener;** *I don't have ...* **no**
tengo ...; *do you have ...?*
¿tiene ...?; *I have to go*
tengo que irme ; *can I*
have ...? **¿me pone ...?**
hay fever **la fiebre del heno**
he **él**
head **la cabeza**
headache **el dolor de cabeza**
headlights **los faros**
headphones **los auriculares**
hear **oír**
hearing aid **el audífono**
heart **el corazón**
hearts (cards) **los corazones**
heater **la estufa**
heating **la calefacción**
heavy **pesado**
hedge **el seto**
heel **el talón;** (shoe) **el tacón**
hello **hola;** (on phone)
dígame
help **la ayuda;** (verb) **ayudar**
hepatitis **la hepatitis**
her: it's for her **es para ella;**
her book **su libro;** *her shoes*
sus zapatos; *it's hers es*
suyo; *give it to her* **déselo**
high **alto**
highway code **el código**
de la circulación
hiking **el senderismo**
hill **el monte**
him: it's for him **es para él;**
give it to him **déselo**
hire (verb) **alquilar**
his: his book **su libro;** *his shoes*
sus zapatos; *it's his* **es suyo**
history **la historia**
hitchhike **hacer auto-stop**
HIV positive **seropositivo**

hobby **el hobby**
holiday **las vacaciones**
home **la casa;**
   at home **en casa**
homeopathy **la homeopatía**
honest **honrado;**
   (sincere) **sincero**
honey **la miel**
honeymoon **el viaje de novios**
horn (car) **el claxon;** (animal)
el cuerno
horrible **horrible**
hospital **el hospital**
hostess **la anfitriona**
hour **la hora**
house **la casa**
household products **los**
   productos del hogar
hovercraft **el aerodeslizador**
how? **¿cómo?**
how are you? **qué tal?**
hundred **cien**
hungry: I'm hungry
   tengo hambre
hurry: I'm in a hurry
   tengo prisa
husband **el marido**
hydrofoil **la hidroaleta**

I

I **yo**
ice **el hielo**
ice cream **el helado**
ice skates
   los patines para hielo
if **si**
ignition **el encendido**
immediately **inmediatamente**
impossible **imposible**
in **en;** in English **en inglés;** in
   the hotel **en el hotel;** in
   Barcelona **en Barcelona;**
   he's not in **no está**
included **incluido**
indicator **el intermitente**
indigestion **indigestión**
inexpensive **barato**
infection **la infección**
information **la información**
inhaler (for asthma etc)
   el spray, el inhalador
injection **la inyección**
injury **la herida**
ink **la tinta**
inn **la fonda**
inner tube
   la cámara (neumática)
insect **el insecto**
insect repellent
   la loción anti-mosquitos

insomnia **el insomnio**
instant coffee
   el café instantáneo
insurance **el seguro**
interesting **interesante**
internet **el internet**
interpret **interpretar**
interpreter **el/la intérprete**
invitation **la invitación**
invoice **la factura**
Ireland **Irlanda**
Irish **irlandés/ irlandesa**
iron (metal) **el hierro;**
   (for clothes) **la plancha;**
   (verb) **planchar**
is **es/está**
island **la isla**
it **lo/la**
Italian (adj) **italiano/**
   italiana (m/f)
Italy **Italia**
its **su**

J

jacket **la chaqueta**
jam **la mermelada**
January **enero**
jazz **el jazz**
jeans **los tejanos,**
   los vaqueros
jellyfish **la medusa**
jeweller's **la joyería**
job **el trabajo**
jog (verb) **hacer footing**
joke **la broma;**
   (funny story) **el chiste**
journey **el viaje**
juice **el zumo**
July **julio**
June **junio**
just (only) **sólo;** it's just arrived
   acaba de llegar

K

kettle **el hervidor de agua**
key **la llave**
keyboard **el teclado**
kidney **el riñón**
kilo **el kilo**
kilometre **el kilómetro**
kitchen **la cocina**
knee **la rodilla**
knife **el cuchillo**
knit **hacer punto**
knitwear
   los artículos de punto
know **saber;** (person,
   place) **conocer;**
   I don't know **no sé**

L

label **la etiqueta**
lace **el encaje**
laces (shoe) **los cordones**
   (de los zapatos)
lady **la señora**
lake **el lago**
lamb **el cordero**
lamp **la lámpara, el flexo**
lampshade **la pantalla**
land **la tierra;**
   (verb) **aterrizar**
language **el idioma**
large **grande**
last (final) **último;**
   at last! **¡por fin!** ; last week
   la semana pasada
late: it's getting late **se está**
   haciendo tarde; the bus is
   late **el autobús se**
   ha retrasado
later **más tarde**
laugh **reír**
laundrette **la lavandería**
   automática
laundry (dirty) **la ropa sucia;**
   (washed) **la colada**
law **el derecho**
lawn **el césped**
lawn mower **la maquina**
   cortacésped
lawyer **el abogado/**
   la abogada
laxative **el laxante**
lazy **perezoso**
lead **la correa**
leaf **la hoja**
leaflet **el folleto**
learn **aprender**
leather **el cuero**
lecture theatre **el anfiteatro**
lecturer (university)
   el profesor/la profesora
   de universidad
left (not right) **izquierdo;**
   there's nothing left
   no queda nada
leg **la pierna**
lemon **el limón**
lemonade **la limonada**
length **la longitud**
lens **la lente**
less **menos**
lesson **la clase**
letter (mail) **la carta;**
   (of alphabet) **la letra**
lettuce **la lechuga**
library **la biblioteca**
licence **el permiso**
life **la vida**

lift **el ascensor**
light **la luz;** (weight) **ligero;** (not dark) **claro**
light bulb **la bombilla**
lighter **el encendedor**
lighter fuel **el gas para el encendedor**
light meter **el fotómetro**
like: I like ... **me gusta ...;** *I like swimming* **me gusta nadar;** *it's like ...* **es como ...;** *like this one* **como éste**
lime (fruit) **la lima**
line **la cola;** (phone etc) **línea;** (verb) **hacer cola**
lipstick **la barra de labios**
liqueur **el licor**
list **la lista**
literature **la literatura**
litre **el litro**
litter **la basura**
little (small) **pequeño;** *it's a little big* **es un poco grande;** *just a little* **sólo un poquito**
liver **el hígado**
living room **el cuarto de estar**
lobster **la langosta**
lollipop **el chupa-chups**
long **largo**
lost property office **la oficina de objetos perdidos**
lot: a lot **mucho**
loud **alto**
lounge (in house) **el cuarto de estar;** (in hotel etc) **el salón**
love **el amor;** (verb) **querer;** *I love Spain* **me encanta España**
lover **el/la amante**
low **bajo**
luck: good luck! **¡suerte!**
luggage **el equipaje**
luggage rack **la rejilla de equipajes**
lunch **la comida**

M

mad **loco**
madam **señora**
magazine **la revista**
mail **el correo**
main course **el plato principal**
main road **la calle principal**
Majorca **Mallorca**
make **hacer**
make-up **el maquillaje**
man **el hombre**

manager **el/la gerente, el jefe;** (hotel) **el director/la directora**
many **muchos/muchas;** *many thanks* **muchas gracias;** *many people* **mucha gente;** *how many* **¿cuántos?;** *too many* **demasiados;** *not many* **no muchos**
map **el mapa;** *town map/plan* **el plano**
marble **el mármol**
March **marzo**
margarine **la margarina**
market **el mercado**
marmalade **la mermelada de naranja**
married **casado**
mascara **el rímel**
mass (church) **la misa**
match (light) **la cerilla;** (sport) **el partido**
material (cloth) **la tela**
matter: it doesn't matter **no importa**
mattress **el colchón**
May **mayo**
maybe **quizás**
me: it's for me **es para mí;** *give it to me* **démelo**
meal **la comida**
mean: what does this mean? **¿qué significa esto?**
meat **la carne**
mechanic **el mecánico**
medicine **la medicina**
Mediterranean **el Mediterráneo**
medium (sherry) **amontillado**
medium-dry (wine) **semi-seco**
meeting **la reunión**
melon **el melón**
menu **la carta;** *set menu* **el menú** (del día)
message **el recado, el mensaje**
metro station **le estación de metro**
microwave **el microondas**
midday **el mediodía**
middle: in the middle **en el centro**
midnight **medianoche**
milk **la leche**
mine: it's mine **es mío**
mineral water **el agua mineral**
minute **el minuto**
mirror **el espejo**
Miss **Señorita**

mistake **la equivocación**
mobile phone **el teléfono móvil, el teléfono celular**
modem **el modem**
Monday **lunes**
money **el dinero**
monitor **el monitor**
month **el mes**
monument **el monumento**
moon **la luna**
moped **el ciclomotor**
more **más**
morning **la mañana;** *in the morning* **por la mañana**
Morocco **Marruecos**
mosaic **el mosaico**
mosquito **el mosquito**
mother **la madre**
motorboat **la motora**
motorcycle **la motocicleta**
motorway **la autopista**
mountain **la montaña**
mountain bike **la bicicleta de montaña**
mouse **el ratón**
mousse (for hair) **la espuma moldeadora**
moustache **el bigote**
mouth **la boca**
move (verb: something) **mover;** (oneself) **moverse;** (house) **mudarse de casa;** *don't move!* **¡no se mueva!**
movie **la película**
Mr **Señor**
Mrs **Señora**
much: much better **mucho mejor;** *much slower* **mucho más despacio**
mug **la jarrita**
Mum **mama**
museum **el museo**
mushrooms **los champiñones, las setas**
music **la música**
musical instrument **el instrumento musical**
musician **el músico**
music system **el equipo de música**
mussels **los mejillones**
must (to have to) **tener que;** *I must ...* **tengo que ...**
mustard **la mostaza**
my: my book **mi libro;** *my keys* **mis llaves**

N

nail (metal) **el clavo**;
   (finger) **la uña**
nail clippers **el cortauñas**
nailfile **la lima de uñas**
nail polish **el esmalte
   de uñas**
name **el nombre**; *what's your
   name?* **¿cómo se llama
   usted?**; *my name is...*
   me llamo...
napkin **la servilleta**
nappy **el pañal**
narrow **estrecho**
near: near the door **junto a
   la puerta**; *near New York*
   cerca de New York
necessary **necesario**
neck **el cuello**
necklace **el collar**
need (verb) **necesitar**;
   I need ... **necesito ...**; *there's
   no need* **no hace falta**
needle **la aguja**
negative (photo) **el negativo**
neither: neither of them
   ninguno de ellos; *neither ...
   nor ...* **ni ... ni ...**
nephew **el sobrino**
never **nunca**
new **nuevo**
news **las noticias**
newsagent's **el kiosko
   de periódicos**
newspaper **el periódico**
New Zealand **Nueva Zelanda**
New Zealander
   **el neozelandés/
   la neozelandesa**
next **próximo, siguiente**;
   next week **la semana que
   viene**; *what next?*
   ¿y ahora qué?
nice **bonito**; (pleasant)
   agradable; (to eat) **bueno**
niece **la sobrina**
night **la noche**
nightclub **la discoteca**
nightgown **el camisón**
night porter
   el vigilante nocturno
nine **nueve**
nineteen **diecinueve**
ninety **noventa**
no (response) **no**; *I have no
   money* **no tengo dinero**
nobody **nadie**
noisy **ruidoso**
noon **mediodía**
north **el norte**

Northern Ireland
   Irlanda del Norte
nose **la nariz**
not **no**; *he's not ...* **no es/está ...**
notebook **el cuaderno**
notepad **el bloc**
nothing **nada**
novel **la novela**
November **noviembre**
now **ahora**
nowhere **en ninguna parte**
nudist **el/la nudista**
number **el número**
number plate **la matrícula**
nurse **el enfermo/la
   enferma**
nut (fruit) **la nuez**;
   (for bolt) **la tuerca**

O

oars **los remos**
occasionally **de vez en cuando**
occupied **ocupado**
October **octubre**
octopus **el pulpo**
of **de**
office (place) **la oficina**;
   (room) **el despacho**
office block **el bloque
   de oficinas**
often **a menudo**
oil **el aceite**
ointment **la pomada**
OK **vale**
old **viejo**; *how old are you?*
   ¿cuántos años tiene?
olive **la aceituna**
olive oil **el aceite de oliva**
olive tree **el olivo**
omelette **la tortilla**
on ... **en ...**
one **uno**
onion **la cebolla**
only **sólo**
open (adj) **abierto**;
   (verb) **abrir**
opening times **el horario
   de apertura**
operating theatre **el quirófano**
operation **la operación**
operator **la operadora**
opposite: opposite the hotel
   enfrente del hotel
optician **el/la oculista**
or **o**
orange (fruit) **la naranja**;
   (colour) **naranja**
orchestra **la orquesta**
order **el pedido**
organ (music) **el órgano**

other: the other (one) **el otro**
our **nuestro**; *it's ours*
   es nuestro
out: he's out **no está**
outside **fuera**; *external* **externa**
oven **el horno**
over ... **encima de ...**; (more
   than) **más de ...**; *it's over
   the road* **está al otro lado
   de la calle**; *when the party
   is over* **cuando termine
   la fiesta**; *over there* **allí**
overtake (in car) **adelantar**
oyster **la ostra**

P

package **el paquete**
packet **el paquete**;
   (cigarettes) **la cajetilla**;
   (sweets, crisps)
   la bolsa
padlock **el candado**
page **la página**
pain **el dolor**
paint **la pintura**
pair **el par**
palace **el palacio**
pale **pálido**
pancakes **las crepes**
paper **el papel**;
   (newspaper) **el periódico**
paraffin **la parafina**
parcel **el paquete**
pardon? **¿cómo dice?**
parents **los padres**
park **el parque**; (verb)
   aparcar; *no parking*
   prohibido aparcar
parsley **el perejil**
parting (hair) **la raya**
party (celebration) **la fiesta**;
   (group) **el grupo**;
   (political) **el partido**
passenger **el pasajero**
passport **el pasaporte**
password **la contraseña**
pasta **la pasta**
path **el camino**
pavement **la acera**
pay **pagar**
payment **el pago**
peach **el melocotón**
peanuts **los cacahuetes**
pear **la pera**
pearl **la perla**
peas **los guisantes**
pedestrian **el peatón**
pedestrian zone **la zona
   peatonal**
peg **la pinza**

pen la pluma
pencil el lápiz
pencil sharpener el sacapuntas
penknife la navaja
pen pal el amigo/la amiga
   por correspondencia
people la gente
pepper la pimienta;
   (red, green) el pimiento
peppermints las pastillas
   de menta
per: per night por noche
perfect perfecto
perfume el perfume
perhaps quizás
perm la permanente
pet passport el pasaporte
   de animales
petrol la gasolina
petrol station la gasolinera
pets los animales
   de compañía; los
   animales domésticos
phone book la guía telefónica
phone booth la cabina
   telefónica
phonecard la tarjeta telefónica
photocopier la fotocopiadora
photograph la foto (grafía);
   (verb) fotografiar
photographer el fotógrafo
phrase book el libro de frases
piano el piano
pickpocket el carterista
picnic el picnic
piece el pedazo
pill la pastilla
pillow la almohada
pilot el piloto
PIN el pin
pin el alfiler
pine (tree) el pino
pineapple la piña
pink rosa
pipe (for smoking) la pipa;
   (for water) la tubería
piston el piston
pitch la plaza
pizza la pizza
place el lugar; at your place
   en su casa
plant la planta
plaster la tirita
plastic el plástico
plastic bag la bolsa de plástico
plastic wrap el plástico
   para envolver
plate el plato
platform (train) el andén
play (theatre) la obra
   de teatro; (verb) jugar

please por favor
pleased to meet you
   encantado/encantada
plug (electrical) el enchufe;
   (sink) el tapón
plumber el fontanero/
   la fontanera
pocket el bolsillo
poison el veneno
police la policía
police officer el policía
police report la denuncia
police station la comisaría
politics la política
poor pobre; (bad quality)
   malo
pop music la música pop
pork la carne de cerdo
port (harbour) el puerto;
   (drink) el oporto
porter (hotel) el conserje
Portugal Portugal
Portuguese portugués
possible posible
post el correo; (verb) echar
   al correo
postbox el buzón
postcard la postal
postcode el código postal
poster el póster
postman el cartero
post office (la oficina de)
   Correos
potato la patata
poultry las aves
pound (sterling) la libra
powder el polvo;
   (cosmetic) los polvos
pram el cochecito
prawns las gambas
prefer preferir
pregnant embarazada
prescription la receta
pretty bonito; (quite) bastante
price el precio
priest el cura
printer la impresora
private privado
problem el problema
profession la profesión
professor el catedrático
profits los beneficios
prohibited prohibido
protection factor (SPF) el
   factor de protección
public público
public holiday el día de
   fiesta
public swimming pool
   la piscina municipal
pull tirar de

puncture el pinchazo
purple morado
purse la cartera,
   el monedero
push empujar
pushchair la sillita de ruedas
put poner
pyjamas el pijama
Pyrenees los Pirineos

Q

quality la calidad
quarter el cuarto
question la pregunta
quick rápido
quiet tranquilo;
   (person) callado
quite (fairly) bastante;
   (fully) completamente

R

rabbit el conejo
radiator el radiador
radio la radio
radish el rábano
rake el rastrillo
railway el ferrocarril
rain la lluvia
raincoat la gabardina
rainforest la selva
raisins las pasas
raspberry la frambuesa
rare (uncommon) raro;
   (steak) poco hecho,
   poco pasado
rat la rata
razor blades
   las cuchillas de afeitar
read leer
ready listo
ready meals
   los platos preparados
receipt el recibo
reception la recepción
receptionist el/
   la recepcionista
record (music) el disco;
   (sport etc) el récord
record player el tocadiscos
record store la tienda de discos
red rojo; (wine) tinto
refreshments los refrescos
refrigerator el frigorífico
registered post
   correo certificado
relative el pariente
relax relajarse; (rest)
   descansar
religion la religión

remember: *I remember* **me acuerdo;** *I don't remember* **no me acuerdo**
repair **arreglar**
report **el informe**
reservation **la reserva**
rest (remainder) **el resto;** (verb: relax) **descansar**
restaurant **el restaurante**
restaurant car **el vagón-restaurante**
return (come back) **volver;** (give back) **devolver**
return ticket **el billete de ida y vuelta**
rice **el arroz**
rich **rico**
right (correct) **correcto;** (not left) **derecho**
ring (for finger) **el anillo**
ripe **maduro**
river **el río**
road **la carretera**
roasted **asado**
robbery **el robo**
rock (stone) **la roca**
roll (bread) **el bollo**
roof **el tejado**
room **la habitación;** (space) **el sitio**
room service **el servicio de habitaciones**
rope **la cuerda**
rose **la rosa**
round (circular) **redondo**
roundabout **la rotonda**
row (verb) **remar**
rowing boat **la barca de remos**
rubber (material) **la goma**
rubber band **la goma**
rubbish **la basura**
ruby (stone) **el rubí**
rug (mat) **la alfombra;** (blanket) **la manta**
rugby **el rugby**
ruins **las ruinas**
ruler (for measuring) **la regla**
rum **el ron**
run (verb) **correr**
runway **la pista**

S

sad **triste**
safe (not dangerous) **seguro**
safety pin **el imperdible**
sailboard **la tabla de windsurfing**
sailing **la vela**
salad **la ensalada**

sale (at reduced prices) **las rebajas**
sales **las ventas**
salmon **el salmón**
salt **la sal**
same: the same dress **el mismo vestido;** *the same people* **la misma gente;** *same again, please* **lo mismo otra vez, por favor**
sand **la arena**
sandals **las sandalias**
sand dunes **las dunas**
sandwich **el bocadillo**
sanitary towels **las compresas**
Saturday **sábado**
sauce **la salsa**
saucepan **el cazo**
saucer **el platillo**
sauna **la sauna**
sausage **la salchicha**
say **decir;** *what did you say?* **¿qué ha dicho?;** *how do you say ...?* **¿cómo se dice ...?**
scampi **las gambas**
scarf **la bufanda;** (head) **el pañuelo**
schedule **el programa**
school **la escuela**
science **las ciencias**
scissors **las tijeras**
Scotland **Escocia**
Scottish **escocés/escocesa**
screen **la pantalla**
screw **el tornillo**
screwdriver **el destornillador**
sea **el mar**
seafood **los mariscos**
seat **el asiento**
seat belt **el cinturón de seguridad**
second **el segundo**
second class **de segunda**
see **ver;** *I can't see* **no veo;** *I see* **comprendo**
self-employed (person) **el autónomo/la autónoma**
sell **vender**
seminar **el seminario**
send **mandar**
separate (adj) **distinto**
separated **separado**
September **septiembre**
serious **serio**
seven **siete**
seventeen **diecisiete**
seventy **setenta**
several **varios**
sew **coser**
shampoo **el champú**

shave **el afeitado;** *to have a shave* **afeitarse**
shaving foam **la espuma de afeitar**
shawl **el chal**
she **ella**
sheet **la sábana;** (of paper) **la hoja**
shell **la concha**
shellfish **mariscos**
sherry **el jerez**
ship **el barco**
shirt **la camisa**
shoelaces **los cordones de los zapatos**
shoe polish **la crema de zapatos**
shoes **los zapatos**
shoe shop **la zapatería**
shop **la tienda**
shopping **la compra;** *to go shopping* **ir de compras**
short **corto;** (height) **bajo**
shorts **los pantalones cortos**
shoulder **el hombro**
shower (bath) **la ducha;** (rain) **el chaparrón**
shower gel **el gel de ducha**
shrimp **las quisquillas**
shutter (camera) **el obturador;** (window) **el postigo**
sick: I feel sick **tengo náuseas;** *to be sick* (vomit) **devolver**
side (edge) **el borde**
side lights **las luces de posición**
sights: the sights of ... **los lugares de interés de ...**
sightseeing **el turismo**
silk **la seda**
silver (metal) **la plata;** (colour) **plateado**
simple **sencillo**
sing **cantar**
single (ticket) **de ida;** (only) **único;** (unmarried) **soltero/soltera**
single room **la habitación** *individual*
sink **el fregadero**
sister **la hermana**
six **seis**
sixteen **dieciséis**
sixty **sesenta**
skid **patinar**
skiing: to go skiing **ir a esquiar**
skin cleanser **la leche limpiadora**
ski resort **la estación de esquí**

skirt la falda
skis los esquís
sky el cielo
sleep el sueño; (verb) dormir
sleeper car el coche-cama
sleeping bag el saco de dormir
sleeping pill el somnífero
sleeve la manga
slip (underwear)
la combinacíon
slippers las zapatillas
slow lento
small pequeño
smell el olor; (verb) oler
smile la sonrisa;
(verb) sonreír
smoke el humo; (verb) fumar
snack la comida ligera
snow la nieve
so: so good tan bueno;
not so much no tanto
soaking solution
(for contact lenses)
la solución limpiadora
soap el jabón
socks los calcetines
soda water la soda
sofa el sofa
soft blando
soil la tierra
somebody alguien
somehow de algún modo
something algo
sometimes a veces
somewhere en alguna parte
son el hijo
song la canción
sorry! ¡perdón!; I'm sorry
perdón/lo siento; sorry?
(pardon) ¿cómo dice?
soup la sopa
south el sur
South America Sudamérica
souvenir el recuerdo
spade la pala
spades (cards) las picas
Spain España
Spaniard el español/
la española
speak hablar;
do you speak ...? ¿habla ...?;
I don't speak ... no hablo ...
speed la velocidad
speed limit el límite de
velocidad
spider la araña
spinach las espinacas
spoon la cuchara
sport el deporte
sports centre
el centro deportivo

spring (mechanical) el muelle;
(season) la primavera
square (in town) la plaza;
(adj) cuadrado
staircase la escalera
stairs las escaleras
stamp el sello
stapler la grapadora
star la estrella
start (beginning) el
principio; (verb) empezar
starters los entrantes
statement la declaración
station la estación
statue la estatua
steak el filete
steal robar; it's been stolen
lo han robado
steamed al vapor
steamer (boat) el vapor
stepdaughter la hijastra
stepfather el padastro
stepmother la madastra
stepson el hijastro
still water el agua sin gas
stockings las medias
stomach el estómago
stomach-ache el dolor
de estómago
stop (bus) la parada; (verb)
parar; stop! ¡alto!
storm la tormenta
strawberries las fresas
stream (small river) el arroyo
street la calle
string la cuerda
stroller la sillita de ruedas
strong fuerte
student el/la estudiante
stupid estúpido
suburbs las afueras
sugar el azúcar
suit (clothing) el traje;
it suits you te sienta bien
suitcase la maleta
sun el sol
sunbathe tomar el sol
sunburn la quemadura de sol
Sunday domingo
sunglasses las gafas de sol
sunny: it's sunny hace sol
sunshade la sombrilla
sunstroke la insolación
suntan: to get a suntan
broncearse
suntan lotion
la loción bronceadora
suntanned bronceado
supermarket el supermercado
supper la cena
supplement el suplemento

suppository el supositorio
sure seguro
surname el apellido
sweat el sudor; (verb) sudar
sweater el jersey
sweatshirt la sudadera
sweet (adj: not sour) dulce;
sweets los caramelos (m)
swim (verb) nadar
swimming la natación
swimming pool la piscina
swimming trunks el bañador
switch el interruptor
synagogue la sinagoga
syringe la jeringuilla
syrup el jarabe

T

table la mesa
tablet la pastilla
take tomar
take off el despegue
talcum powder
los polvos de talco
talk la charla; (verb) hablar
tall alto
tampons los tampones
tangerine la mandarina
tap el grifo
tapestry el tapiz
taxi el taxi
taxi rank la parada de taxis
tea el té
teacher el profesor/
la profesora
technician el técnico
telephone el teléfono; (verb)
llamar por teléfono
television la televisión
temperature la temperatura;
(fever) la fiebre
ten diez
tennis el tenis
tent la tienda (de campaña)
tent peg
la estaquilla, la estaca
tent pole el mástil
terminal el terminal
terrace la terraza
test la prueba
than que
thank (verb) agradecer;
thank you/thanks gracias;
that ese/esa, eso;
that bus ese autobús;
that man ese hombre;
that woman esa mujer;
what's that? ¿qué es eso?;
I think that ... creo que ...;
that one ése/ésa

the el/la; (plural) los/las
theatre el teatro
their: their room su habitación; their books sus libros; it's theirs es suyo
them: it's for them es para ellos/ellas; give it to them déselo
then entonces; (after) después
there allí; there is/are ... hay ...; is/are there ...? ¿hay ...?
these: these men estos hombres; these women estas mujeres; these are mine éstos son míos
they ellos/ellas
thick grueso
thief el ladrón
thin delgado
think pensar; I think so creo que sí; I'll think about it lo pensaré
third tercero
thirsty: I'm thirsty tengo sed
thirteen trece
thirty treinta
this: this one éste/ésta; this man este hombre; this woman esta mujer; what's this? ¿qué es esto?; this is Mr ... éste es el señor ...
those: those men esos hombres; those women esas mujeres
thousand mil
throat la garganta
through por
three tres
thunderstorm la tormenta
Thursday jueves
ticket (train etc) el billete; (theatre etc) la entrada
ticket office la taquilla
tide la marea
tie la corbata; (verb) atar
tight ajustado
tights las medias, los pantis
time tiempo; what's the time? ¿qué hora es?
timetable el horario
tin la hojalata
tip (end) la punta; (money) la propina
tired cansado
tissues los pañuelos de papel
to: to America a América; to the station a la estación; to the doctor al médico
toast la tostada

tobacco el tabaco
tobacconist el estanco
today hoy
together juntos
toilet (room in house) el baño; (bathroom item) el váter; (in public establishment) los servicos
toilet paper el papel higiénico
toilets (men) los servicios de caballeros; (women) los servicios de señoras
tomato el tomate
tomato juice el zumo de tomate
tomorrow mañana
tongue la lengua
tonic la tónica
tonight esta noche
too (also) también; (excessively) demasiado
tooth el diente; back tooth la muela
toothache el dolor de muelas
toothbrush el cepillo de dientes
toothpaste la pasta dentífrica
torch la linterna
tour la excursión
tourist el/la turista
tourist office la oficina de turismo
towel la toalla
tower la torre
town el pueblo
town hall el ayuntamiento
toy el juguete
trade fair la feria
track suit el chandal
tractor el tractor
tradition la tradición
traffic el tráfico
traffic jam el atasco
traffic lights el semáforo
trailer la caravana, el remolque
train el tren
trainee el aprendiz
trainers los zapatos de deporte
translate traducir
translator el traductor/ la traductora
travel agency la agencia de viajes
traveller's cheque el cheque de viaje
tray la bandeja
tree el árbol
trolley el carrito

trousers el pantalón
truck el camión
true cierto; it's true es verdad
try intentar
Tuesday martes
tunnel el túnel
turn (left/right) tuerza (a la izquierda/ a la derecha)
turn: it's my turn me toca a mí
tweezers las pinzas
twelve doce
twenty veinte
two dos
typewriter la máquina de escribir
tyre el neumático

U

ugly feo
umbrella el paraguas
uncle el tío
under ... debajo de ...
underground (railway) el metro
underpants los calzoncillos
understand entender; I don't understand no entiendo
underwear la ropa interior
United States Estados Unidos
university la universidad
unleaded sin plomo
until hasta
unusual poco común
up arriba; (upward) hacia arriba
urgent urgente
us: it's for us es para nosotros/nosotras; give it to us dénoslo
use el uso; (verb) usar; it's no use no sirve de nada
useful útil
usual corriente
usually en general

V

vacancies (rooms) habitaciones libres
vaccination la vacuna
vacuum cleaner la aspiradora
valley el valle
valve la válvula
vanilla la vainilla
vase el jarrón
veal la (carne de) ternera

vegetables **la verdura**
vegetarian **vegetariano**
vehicle **el vehículo**
very **muy;** *very much* **mucho**
vest **la camiseta**
vet **el veterinario**
video (tape) **la cinta de vídeo;** (film) **el vídeo**
video games **los vídeo-juegos**
video recorder **el (aparato de) vídeo**
view **la vista**
viewfinder **el visor de imagen**
villa **el chalet**
village **el pueblo**
vinegar **el vinagre**
violin **el violín**
visit **la visita; visitar** (verb)
visiting hours **las horas de visita**
visitor **el/la visitante**
vitamin pills **las vitaminas**
vodka **el vodka**
voice **la voz**
voicemail **la mensajería de voz**

W

wait **esperar;** *wait!* **¡espere!**
waiter **el camarero;** *waiter!* **¡camarero!**
waiting room **la sala de espera**
waitress **la camarera;** *waitress!* **¡Oiga,** *por favor!*
Wales **Gales**
walk (stroll) **el paseo;** (verb) **andar;** *to go for a walk* **ir de paseo**
wall **la pared;** (outside) **el muro**
wallet **la cartera**
want (verb) **querer**
war **la guerra**
wardrobe **el armario**
warm **caliente;** (weather) **caluroso**
was **estaba/era**
washing machine **la zapatilla**
washing powder **el jabón de lavadora, el detergente**
washing-up liquid **el lavavajillas**
wasp **la avispa**
watch **el reloj;** (verb) **mirar**
water **el agua**
waterfall **la cascada**
water heater **el calentador** (de agua)

wave **la ola;** (verb) **agitar**
wavy (hair) **ondulado**
we **nosotros/nosotras**
weather **el tiempo**
website **la web site, el sitio web**
wedding **la boda**
Wednesday **miércoles**
weeds **las malas hierbas**
week **la semana**
welcome (adj) **bienvenido;** (verb) **dar la bienvenida;** *you're welcome* **no hay de qué**
wellington boots **las botas de agua**
Welsh **galés/galesa**
were: you were (informal singular) **eras/estabas;** (formal singular) **era/estaba;** (informal plural) **erais/estabais;** (formal plural) **eran/estaban;** *we were* **éramos/estábamos;** *they were* **eran/estaban**
west **el oeste**
wet **mojado**
what? **¿qué?**
wheel **la rueda**
wheel brace **la llave de las tuercas**
wheelchair **la silla de ruedas**
when? **¿cuándo?**
where? **¿dónde?**
whether **si**
which? **¿cuál?**
whisky **el whisky**
white **blanco**
white coffee **el café con leche**
who? **¿quién?**
why? **¿por qué?**
wide **ancho;** *3 metres wide* **de tres metros de anchura**
wife **la mujer**
wind **el viento**
window **la ventana**
windscreen **el parabrisas**
wine **el vino**
wine list **la carta de vinos**
wine merchant **el vinatero**
wing **el ala**
with **con**
without **sin**
witness **el testigo**
woman **la mujer**
wood (material) **la madera**
wool **la lana**
word **la palabra**

work **el trabajo;** (verb) **trabajar;** (to function) **funcionar**
worktop **el mostrador**
worse **peor**
worst **(el) peor**
wrapping paper **el papel de envolver;** (for presents) **el papel de regalo**
wrench **la llave inglesa**
wrist **la muñeca**
writing paper **el papel de escribir**
wrong **equivocado**

X, Y, Z

x-ray department **el servicio de radiología**
year **el año**
yellow **amarillo**
yes **sí**
yesterday **ayer**
yet **todavía;** *not yet* **todavía no**
yoghurt **el yogur**
you (informal singular) **tú;** (formal singular) **usted;** (informal plural, m/f) **vosotros/ vosotras;** (formal plural) **ustedes**
young **joven**
your: your book (informal singular) **tu libro;** (formal singular) **su libro;** *your shoes* (informal singular) **tus zapatos;** (formal singular) **sus zapato**
yours: is this yours? (informal) **¿es tuyo esto?;** (formal) **¿es suyo esto?**
youth hostel **el albergue juvenil**
zip **la cremallera**
zoo **el zoo**

DICTIONARY
Spanish to English

The gender of Spanish nouns listed here is indicated by the abbreviations (m) for masculine nouns and (f) for feminine nouns. Plural nouns are followed by the abbreviations (m pl) or (f pl). Spanish adjectives (adj) vary according to the gender and number of the word they describe, and the masculine form is shown here. In general, adjectives that end in **-o** adopt an **-a** ending in the feminine form, and those that end in **-e** usually stay the same. For the plural form, **-s** is added.

A

a to; **a América** to America; **a la estación** to the station; **al médico** to the doctor; **a las tres** at 3 o'clock
abanico (m) fan (handheld)
abierto open (adj)
abogado/abogada (m/f) lawyer
abrebotellas (m) bottle opener
abrelatas (m) can opener
abrigo (m) coat
abril April
abrir to open
abuela (f) grandmother
abuelo (m) grandfather
abuelos (m pl) grandparents
aburrido boring
acaba de llegar it's just arrived
accidente (m) accident
aceite (m) oil; **el aceite de oliva** olive oil
aceituna (f) olive
acelerador (m) accelerator
acera (f) pavement
acondicionador (m) conditioner (hair)
acuerdo: me acuerdo I remember; **no me acuerdo** I don't remember
adaptador (m) adaptor
adelantar overtake (car)
adiós goodbye
aduana (f) customs
aerodeslizador (m) hovercraft
aeropuerto (m) airport
afeitado (m) shave; **afeitarse** to have a shave
after-shave (m) aftershave
afueras (f pl) suburbs
agencia (f) agency

agencia de viajes (f) travel agency
agenda (f) diary
agitar to wave
agosto August
agradable pleasant
agradecer to thank
agua (m) water; **el agua con gas** fizzy water; **el agua mineral** mineral water; **el agua potable** drinking water; **el agua sin gas** still water
aguja (f) needle
ahora now; **¿y ahora qué?** what next?
aire (m) air
aire acondicionado (m) air conditioning
ajedrez (m) chess
ajo (m) garlic
ajustado tight
ala (m) wing
albañil (m) builder
albaricoque (m) apricot
albergue juvenil (m) youth hostel
alcachofa (f) artichoke
alcohol (m) alcohol
alegre glad
alemán German
Alemania Germany
alérgico allergic
alfiler (m) pin
alfombra (f) carpet; rug
algo something
algodón (m) cotton, cotton wool
alguien somebody
alguna: en alguna parte somewhere
allí there, over there
almohada (f) pillow
alojamiento (m) accommodation
alquilar to hire

alto high, tall, loud
¡alto! stop!
amante (m/f) lover
amargo bitter
amarillo yellow
ambulancia (f) ambulance
América America
americano/americana (m/f) American
amigo/amiga (m/f) friend; **amigo/amiga por correspondencia** (m/f) pen pal
amontillado medium (sherry)
amor (m) love
ampliación (f) enlargement
ampolla (f) blister
análisis de sangre (m) blood test
andar to walk
andén (m) platform
anfiteatro (m) lecture theatre
anfitriona (f) hostess
anillo (m) ring (jewellery)
animal (m) animal; **los animales de compañía/los animales domésticos** pets
año (m) year
antes de ... before ...
anticonceptivo (m) contraceptive
anticongelante (m) antifreeze
anticuario (m) antique shop
antiséptico (m) antiseptic
aparcamiento (m) car park
aparcar to park; **prohibido aparcar** no parking
apartamento (m) apartment
apellido (m) surname
aperitivo (m) aperitif
apetito (m) appetite
aprender learn

aprendiz (m) *trainee*
apretón de manos (m) *handshake*
araña (f) *spider*
árbol (m) *tree*
árbol de levas (m) *camshaft*
arcón (m) *chest* (furniture)
arena (f) *sand*
Argelia *Algeria*
armario (m) *cupboard, wardrobe*
arreglar *repair*
arriba *up;* **hacia arriba** *upward*
arroyo (m) *stream* (small river)
arroz (m) *rice*
arte (m) *art*
artículos de punto (m pl) *knitwear*
artista (m/f) *artist*
asado *roasted*
ascensor (m) *lift*
asiento (m) *seat;* **el asiento infantil** *car seat* (for a baby/child)
asistenta (f) *cleaner*
asmático *asthmatic*
aspiradora (f) *vacuum cleaner*
aspirina (f) *aspirin*
atar *to tie*
atasco (m) *traffic jam*
aterrizar *to land*
ático (m) *attic*
atractivo *attractive* (offer)
audífono (m) *hearing aid*
auriculares (m pl) *headphones*
Australia *Australia*
australiano/australiana (m/f) *Australian*
autobús (m) *bus;* **autobús del aeropuerto** *airport bus*
autocaravana (f) *camper van*
automático *automatic*
autónomo/autónoma (m/f) *self-employed*
autopista (f) *motorway*
avería (f) *(car) breakdown;* **he tenido una avería** *I've had a breakdown*
aves (f pl) *poultry*
avión (m) *aircraft*
avispa (f) *wasp*
ayer *yesterday*
ayuda (f) *help*
ayudar *to help*
ayuntamiento (m) *town hall*
azúcar (m) *sugar*
azul *blue*

B

bacon (m) *bacon*
bailar *to dance*
baile (m) *dance*
bajarse *to get off* (bus etc); *to get out*
bajo *low, short*
balandro (m) *sailing boat*
balcón (m) *balcony*
Baleares: las (Islas) **Baleares** *Balearic Islands*
balón (m) *football (ball);* **el balón de playa** *beach ball*
baloncesto (m) *basketball*
bañador (m) *bathing suit, swimming trunks*
banco (m) *bank*
banda (f) *band* (musicians)
bandeja (f) *tray*
bandera (f) *flag*
baño (m) *bath, bathroom, toilet* (room in a house); **darse un baño** *to have a bath;* **el traje de baño** *bathing suit*
bar (m) *bar* (drinks)
baraja (f) *deck of cards*
barato *inexpensive*
barba (f) *beard*
barbacoa (f) *barbecue*
barca (f) *small boat;* **la barca de remos** *rowing boat*
barco (m) *boat, ship*
barra de labios (f) *lipstick*
bastante *enough, quite, fairly*
basura (f) *litter, rubbish*
batería (f) *battery* (car)
bebé (m) *baby*
beber *to drink;* **¿quiere beber algo?** *would you like something to drink?*
bebida (f) *drink*
beige *beige*
beneficios (m pl) *profits*
berenjenas (f pl) *aubergines*
biblioteca (f) *library*
bicicleta (f) *bicycle;* **la bicicleta de montaña** *mountain bike*
bien *good;* **te sienta bien** *it suits you*
bienvenido *welcome*
bigote (m) *moustache*
billete (m) *fare, ticket* (train etc); **billete de ida y vuelta** (m) *return ticket*

billete de banco (m) *banknote*
bizcocho (m) *sponge cake*
blanco *white*
blando *soft*
bloc (m) *notepad*
bloque de oficinas (m) *office block*
blusa (f) *blouse*
boca (f) *mouth*
bocadillo (m) *sandwich*
boda (f) *wedding*
bodega (f) *cellar*
bolígrafo (m) *ballpoint pen*
bollo (m) *roll* (bread)
bolsa (f) *bag, packet* (sweets, crisps); **la bolsa de basura** *bin liner;* **la bolsa de plástico** *plastic bag*
bolsillo (m) *pocket*
bolso (m) *handbag*
bombilla (f) *light bulb*
bonito *nice, pretty, attractive* (object)
bordado (m) *embroidery*
borde (m) *edge, border, side*
borracho *drunk*
bosque (m) *forest*
bota (f) *boot*
botas de agua (f pl) *wellington boots*
botella (f) *bottle*
botón (m) *button*
brazo (m) *arm*
bridge (m) *bridge (game)*
británico/británica (m/f) *British*
brocha (f) *paint brush*
broche (m) *brooch*
broma (f) *joke*
bronceado *suntanned*
broncearse *suntan: to get a suntan*
buenas noches *good evening*
buenas tardes *good afternoon*
bueno *good, good to eat, tasty*
buenos días *good morning*
bufanda (f) *scarf*
buzón (m) *postbox*

C

cabeza (f) *head*
cabina telefónica (f) *phone booth*
cable alargador (m) *extension cord*
cacahuetes (m pl) *peanuts*
cada *every, each;* **veinte euros cada uno** *20 euros each*

café (m) *café, coffee;*
  el café con leche
  white coffee; **el café**
  instantáneo *instant coffee;*
  el café solo *espresso*
caja (f) *box; check-out;* **la caja**
  de bombones *box of*
  chocolates; **la caja de**
  cambios *gearbox*
cajero (m) *cashier;*
  el cajero automático
  ATM, cashpoint
cajetilla (f) *packet (cigarettes)*
calambre (m) *cramp*
calcetines (m pl) *socks*
calculadora (m) *calculator*
calefacción (f) *heating;*
  la calefacción central
  central heating
calentador (de agua) (m)
  water heater
calidad (f) *quality*
caliente *warm*
callado *quiet (person)*
calle (f) *street;* **la calle**
  principal *main road*
caluroso *warm (weather)*
calzoncillos (m pl) *underpants*
cama (f) *bed*
cámara de fotos (f) *camera*
cámara neumática (f)
  inner tube
camarera (f) *waitress*
camarero (m) *waiter;*
  ¡camarero! *waiter!*
cambiar *to change* (money)
cambiarse *to change* (clothes)
cambio (m) *change (money);*
  exchange rate
camino (m) *path*
camión (m) *truck*
camisa (f) *shirt*
camiseta (f) *vest*
camisón (m) *nightgown*
campana (f) *bell* (church)
camping (m) *campsite*
camping-gas (m) *camping gas*
campo (m) *countryside, field*
Canadá *Canada*
canadiense *Canadian*
canal (m) *canal*
Canarias: las (Islas)
  Canarias Canaries
canción (f) *song*
candado (m) *padlock*
cangrejo (m) *crab*
cansado *tired*
cantar *to sing*
capazo (m) *crib*
capó (m) *bonnet (car)*
cara (f) *face*

caramelos (m) *sweets*
caravana (f) *trailer*
carburador (m) *carburetor*
cardenal (m) *bruise*
cargador (m) *charger*
carne (f) *meat*
carne de cerdo (f) *pork*
carne de vaca (f) *beef*
carnet de conducir (m)
  driving licence
carnicería (f) *butcher's*
caro *expensive*
carpintero (m) *carpenter*
carretera (f) *road*
carrito (m) *trolley*
carta (f) *letter* (mail); *menu;* **la**
  carta de vinos (f) *wine list*
cartera (f) *purse, briefcase,*
  wallet
carterista (m) *pickpocket*
cartero (m) *postman*
casa (f) *house, home;*
  en casa *at home*
casado *married*
cascada (f) *waterfall*
casi *almost*
cassette (f) *cassette*
castaño *brown (hair)*
castañuelas (f pl) *castanets*
castellano *Castilian*
Castilla *Castile*
castillo (m) *castle*
Cataluña *Catalonia*
catedral (f) *cathedral*
catedrático (m) *professor*
católico *Catholic* (adj)
catorce *fourteen*
cazo (m) *saucepan*
cebo (m) *bait*
cebolla (f) *onion*
ceja (f) *eyebrow*
cementerio (m) *cemetery*
cena (f) *dinner, supper,*
  dinner party
cenicero (m) *ashtray*
centro (m) *centre; city centre;*
  el centro deportivo *sports*
  centre; **en el centro**
  middle: in the middle
cepillar el pelo *to brush hair*
cepillo (m) *brush (for cleaning);*
  el cepillo del pelo *hair*
  brush; **el cepillo de**
  dientes *toothbrush*
cerca *near, close;* (f) *fence*
cereza (f) *cherry*
cerilla (f) *match (light)*
cerrado *closed*
cerrar *to close*
cerrojo (m) *bolt (on door)*
certificado (m) *certificate*

cerveza (f) *beer*
césped (m) *lawn*
cesto (m) *basket*
chal (m) *shawl*
chalet (m) *villa*
champiñones (m pl)
  mushrooms
champú (m) *shampoo*
chandal (m) *track suit*
chaparrón (m) *shower (rain)*
chaqueta (f) *jacket*
charcutería (f) *delicatessen*
charla (f) *talk*
cheque (m) *cheque;*
  el cheque de viaje
  traveller's cheque
chica (f) *girl*
chicle (m) *chewing gum*
chico (m) *boy*
chimenea (f) *chimney,*
  fireplace
chincheta (f) *drawing pin*
chiste (m) *joke (funny story)*
chocolate (m) *chocolate*
chuleta (f) *chop (food)*
chupa-chups (m) *lollipop*
ciclismo (m) *cycling*
ciclomotor (m) *moped*
ciego *blind (cannot see)*
cielo (m) *sky*
cien *hundred*
ciencias (f pl) *science*
cierto *true*
cigalas (f pl) *crayfish*
cigarrillo (m) *cigarette*
cinco *five*
cincuenta *fifty*
cine (m) *cinema*
cinta (f) *cassette;* **el cinta**
  de vídeo *video tape*
cinturón (m) *belt;* **el cinturón**
  de seguridad *seat belt*
cita (f) *appointment*
ciudad (f) *city, town;*
  el centro ciudad *city centre*
claro *clear (water); light*
  (adj: not dark)
clase (f) *class; lesson*
clavo (m) *nail (metal)*
claxon (m) *horn (car)*
cliente (m) *client*
cobrador (m) *conductor (bus)*
cobrar *to cash*
cocer *to cook, boil*
cocer al horno *to bake*
coche (m) *car*
coche-cama (m) *sleeper car*
cochecito (m) *pram*
cocina (f) *cooker; kitchen*
cocinero/cocinera (m/f) *cook*
coctel (m) *cocktail party*

código code; **el código de la circulación** highway code; **el código** postal postcode
codo (m) elbow
coger catch; **coger el tren** to catch the train
cojín (m) cushion
col (f) cabbage
cola (f) line
colada (f) laundry (washed)
colcha (f) bedspread
colchón (m) mattress
colchoneta (f) air mattress
colección (f) collection (stamps etc)
coliflor (f) cauliflower
collar (m) collar (of animal)
collar (m) necklace; colour
combinacíon (f) slip (underwear)
comedor (m) dining room
comer to eat
comida (f) food, meal; lunch
comida ligera (f) snack
comisaría (f) police station
como like; **como éste** like this one
¿cómo? how?; **¿cómo se llama usted?** what's your name?**¿cómo dice?** pardon?, what did you say?
cómoda (f) chest of drawers
compañía aérea (f) airline
compartimento (m) compartment
completamente completely
complicado complicated
compra (f) shopping
comprar to buy
comprendo I see
compresas (f pl) sanitary towels
con with
coñac (m) brandy
concha (f) shell
concierto (m) concert
concurrido crowded
condón (m) condom
conducir to drive
conductor (m) driver
conejo (m) rabbit
conferencia (f) conference; **la sala de conferencias** conference room
congelador (m) freezer
congelados (m pl) frozen foods
conocer to know (person, place)
conserje (m) porter (hotel)
consulado (m) consulate
contable (m/f) accountant
contendor de basura (m) bin
contento happy

contestador automático (m) answering machine
contra against
contraseña (f) password
contrato (m) contract
copa (f) glass (for drinking)
corazón (m) heart
corazones (m pl) hearts (cards)
corbata (f) tie
corcho (m) cork
cordero (m) lamb
cordones (de los zapatos) (m pl) (shoe)laces
correa (f) lead
correcto right (correct)
correo (m) mail, post; **el correo certificado** registered post; **el correo electrónico** email
Correos: (la oficina de) **Correos** (f) post office
correr to run
corrida de toros (f) bullfight
corriente ordinary; usual
cortadura (f) cut
cortar to chop, cut
cortauñas (m) nail clippers
corte de pelo (m) haircut
cortina (f) curtain
corto short
coser to sew
cosméticos (m pl) cosmetics
costar to cost; **¿cuánto cuesta?** what does it cost?
crema (f) cream (lotion)
crema de zapatos (f) shoe polish
cremallera (f) zip
creo que ... I think that ...
crepes (f pl) pancakes
crisis nerviosa (f) nervous breakdown
cristal (m) glass (material)
crucero (m) cruise
cuaderno (m) notebook
cuadrado square (adj)
¿cuál? which?
cualquiera de ellos either of them
¿cuándo? when?
¿cuánto cuesta? what does it cost?, how much is it?
¿cuántos años tiene? how old are you?
cuarenta forty
cuarto (m) quarter, room; (adj) fourth
cuarto de baño (m) bathroom
cuarto de estar (m) living room, lounge
cuatro four

cubo (m) bucket; **el cubo de la basura** dustbin
cucaracha (f) cockroach
cuchara (f) spoon
cuchillas de afeitar (f pl) razor blades
cuchillo (m) knife
cuello (m) neck, collar
cuenco (m) bowl
cuenta (f) bill
cuerda (f) string; rope
cuerno (m) horn (animal)
cuero (m) leather
cuerpo (m) body
cueva (f) cave
¡cuidado! be careful!
cumpleaños (m) birthday
cuna (f) cot
cura (m) priest
curry (m) curry

D

dar give; **dar la bienvenida** to welcome
de of; **de algún** modo somehow; **de ida** single (ticket)
debajo de below, under
decir say; **¿qué ha dicho?** what did you say?; **¿cómo se dice ...?** how do you say ...?
declaración (f) statement
dedo (m) finger
delante de in front of ...
delgado thin
demasiado too (excessively)
démelo give it to me
dentadura postiza (f) dentures, false teeth
dentista (m/f) dentist
denuncia (f) police report
departamento (m) department
deporte (m) sport
derecho (m) law, justice; **no hay derecho** it's not fair; (adj) right (not left)
desayuno (m) breakfast
descansar to rest
descuento (m) discount
desmayarse to faint
desodorante (m) deodorant
despacho (m) office (room)
despegue (m) take off
despertador (m) alarm clock
después then (after); **después de ...** after ...
destornillador (m) screwdriver
detergente (m) washing powder
detrás de ... behind ...
devolver to return (give back); to be sick (vomit)

día (m) *day*; **el día de fiesta** *public holiday*
diabético *diabetic*
diamantes (m pl) *diamonds*
diarrea (f) *diarrhoea*
diccionario (m) *dictionary*
diciembre *December*
diecinueve *nineteen*
dieciocho *eighteen*
dieciséis *sixteen*
diecisiete *seventeen*
diente (m) *tooth*
diesel *diesel* (adj: engine)
diez *ten*
diferente *different*
difícil *difficult*
dígame *hello* (on phone)
dinero (m) *money, cash*; **no tengo dinero** *I have no money*
dirección (f) *address*
director/directora (m/f) *manager* (hotel); *conductor* (orchestra)
disco (m) *record* (music)
disco compacto (m) *compact disc*
discoteca (f) *nightclub*
diseñador/diseñadora (m/f) *designer*
disponible *available*
distancia *distance*; **¿qué distancia hay a ...?** *how far is it to ...?*
distinto *separate, different* (adj); **¡eso es distinto!** *that's different!*; **quería otro distinto** *I'd like a different one*
diversiones (f pl) *entertainment*
divertido; (odd) **raro** *funny*
divorciado *divorced*
doce *twelve*
documento (m) *document*
dólar (m) *dollar*
dolor (m) *ache, pain*; **el dolor de cabeza** *headache*; **el dolor de estómago** *stomach-ache*; **el dolor de muelas** *toothache*
domingo *Sunday*
¿dónde? *where?*; **¿dónde está ...?** *where is ...?*
dónut (m) *doughnut*
dormir *to sleep*
dormitorio (m) *bedroom*
dos *two*; **los dos** *both*
ducha (f) *shower* (bath)
dulce *sweet* (adj: not sour)

dunas (f pl) *sand dunes*
durante *during*
duro *hard* (not soft)
duty-free (m) *duty-free shop*

E

echar al correo *to post*
echar el cerrojo *to bolt*
edificio (m) *building*
edredón (m) *duvet*
eje (m) *axle*
ejecutivo (m) *executive*
ejemplo (m) *example*; **por ejemplo** *for example*
él *he, him, the* (m); **es para él** *it's for him*
elástico *elastic*
electricidad (f) *electricity*
electricista (m/f) *electrician*
eléctrico *electric*
ella *she, her, the* (f); **es para ella** *it's for her*
ellos/ellas *they, them*; **es para ellos/ellas** *it's for them*
email (m) *email*; **la dirección de email** *email address*
embajada (f) *embassy*
embarazada *pregnant*
embarazoso *embarrassing*
emergencia (f) *emergency*
empaste (m) *filling* (in tooth)
empezar *to start*
empleado (m) *employee*
empujar *to push*
en *on, at, in*; **en inglés** *in English*; **en el hotel** *in the hotel*; **en Barcelona** *in Barcelona*; **en Correos** *at the post office*; **en su casa** *at your place*
encaje (m) *lace*
encantado/encantada (m/f) *pleased to meet you*
encargado (m) *caretaker*
encendedor (m) *lighter*
encendido (m) *ignition*
enchufe (m) *plug* (electrical)
encima de ... *over ...*
encuentro (m) *meeting*; **no me encuentro bien** *I don't feel well*
enero *January*
enfermo/enferma (m/f) *nurse*
enfrente de *opposite*; **enfrente del hotel** *opposite the hotel*
¡enhorabuena! *congratulations!*
ensalada (f) *salad*

entender *to understand*; **no entiendo** *I don't understand*
entonces *then, so*
entrada (f) *entrance, ticket* (theatre etc)
entrantes (m pl) *starters*
entre ... *between ...*
entrega (f) *delivery*
enviar por fax *to fax*
epiléptico *epileptic*
equipaje (m) *luggage*; **el equipaje de mano** *hand luggage*
equipo de música (m) *music system*
equivocación (f) *mistake*
equivocado *wrong*
era *you were* (formal): *it/he/she was*
éramos *we were*
eran *they were*
eras *you were* (informal)
eres *you are* (informal)
es *you are* (formal)
es *it/he/she is*
escalera (f) *staircase*; **la escalera mecánica** *escalator*; **las escaleras** *stairs*
escarcha (f) *frost*
escocés/escocesa (m/f) *Scottish*
Escocia *Scotland*
escopeta (f) *gun* (rifle)
escuela (f) *school*
ese/esa *that*; **ese autobús** *that bus*; **ese hombre** *that man*; **esa mujer** *that woman*; **¿qué es eso?** *what's that?*
ése/ésa *that, that one*;
esmalte de uñas (m) *nail polish*
esos/esas *those, those ones*; **esos hombres** *those men*; **esas mujeres** *those women*
espalda (f) *back* (body)
España *Spain*
español/española (m/f) *Spanish, Spaniard*
especialidad (f) *field of study*
espejo (m) *mirror*
esperar *to wait*; **¡espere!** *wait!*
espinacas (f pl) *spinach*
espuma de afeitar (f) *shaving foam*
espuma moldeadora (f) *mousse* (for hair)
esquina (f) *corner* (of street)

esquís (m pl) *skis*
está *you are* (formal)
está *it/he/she is*
esta noche *tonight*
estaba *it/he/she was; you were* (formal)
estábamos *we were*
estaban *they were*
estabas *you were* (informal)
estaca (f) *tent peg*
estación (f) *station;* la estación de autobuses *bus station;* la estación de esquí *ski resort;* la estación de metro *metro station*
Estados Unidos *United States*
estamos *we are*
están *they are*
estanco (m) *tobacconist*
estaquilla (f) *tent peg*
estás *you are* (informal)
estatua (f) *statue*
este *east;* el Este *the East*
éste/ésta *this, this one;* este hombre *this man;* esta mujer *this woman;* ¿qué es esto? *what's this?;* éste es el señor ... *this is Mr ...*
estómago (m) *stomach*
estos/estas *these, these ones;* estos hombres *these men;* estas mujeres *these women;* éstos son míos *these are mine*
estoy *I am*
estrecho *narrow* (adj)
estrella (f) *star*
estudiante (m/f) *student*
estufa (f) *heater*
estúpido *stupid*
etiqueta (f) *label*
evidente *clear* (obvious)
excelente *excellent*
exceso de equipaje (m) *excess baggage*
excursión (f) *excursion, tour*
exposición (f) *exhibition*
externa *external*
extintor (m) *fire extinguisher*
extranjero/extranjera (m/f) *foreigner*

F

fácil *easy*
factor de protección (m) *protection factor* (SPF)
factura (f) *invoice*
facturación (f) *check-in*
facturar *to check in*
falda (f) *skirt*
falta: no hace falta *there's no need*
familia (f) *family*
fan (m) *fan* (enthusiast)
fantástico *fantastic*
farmacia (f) *chemist*
faros (m pl) *headlights*
fax (m) *fax*
febrero *February*
¡felicidades! *happy birthday!*
feliz *happy*
feo *ugly*
feria (f) *fair, trade fair*
ferretería (f) *hardware store*
ferrocarril (m) *railway*
ferry (m) *ferry*
fiebre (f) *temperature,* fever; la fiebre del heno *hay fever*
fiesta (f) *party* (celebration)
filete (m) *steak*
filtro (m) *filter*
fin (m) *end;* ¡por fin! *at last!*
final (m) *end*
fino *dry* (sherry)
flash (m) *flash* (camera)
flauta (f) *flute*
flequillo (m) *fringe* (hair)
flexo (m) *angle-poise lamp*
flor (f) *flower*
folleto (m) *brochure, leaflet*
fonda (f) *inn*
fondo (m) *bottom*
fontanero/fontanera (m/f) *plumber*
foto (grafía) (f) *photograph*
fotocopiadora (f) *photocopier*
fotografiar *to photograph*
fotógrafo (m) *photographer*
fotómetro (m) *light meter*
frambuesa (f) *raspberry*
francés *French*
Francia *France*
fregadero (m) *sink*
freír *to fry*
frenar *to brake*
freno (m) *brake;* el freno de emergencia *emergency brake;* el freno de mano *handbrake*
fresas (f pl) *strawberries*
fresco *cool*
frigorífico (m) *fridge*
frío *cold* (adj); *I'm cold* tengo frío
frito *fried*
frontera (f) *border* (between countries)
fruta (f) *fruit*

fuego (m) *fire;* los fuegos artificiales *fireworks*
fuel-oil *diesel* (oil)
fuente (f) *fountain*
fuera *outside*
fuerte *strong*
fumar *to smoke*
funcionar *to work* (function)
fútbol (m) *football* (game)

G

gabardina (f) *raincoat*
gafas (f pl) *glasses;* las gafas de sol *sunglasses*
galería de arte (f) *art gallery*
Gales *Wales*
galés/galesa *Welsh*
galleta (f) *biscuit*
gambas (f pl) *prawns*
ganga (f) *bargain*
garage (m) *garage* (for parking)
garantía (f) *guarantee*
garantizar *to guarantee*
garganta (f) *throat*
gas para el encendedor (m) *lighter fuel*
gasolina (f) *petrol*
gasolinera (f) *petrol station*
gato (m) *cat*
gay *gay* (homosexual)
gel (m) *gel* (hair); el gel de ducha *shower gel*
gemelos (m pl) *cuff links*
general: en general *usually*
gente (f) *people*
gerente (m/f) *manager*
Gibraltar *Gibraltar*
ginebra (f) *gin*
gobierno (m) *government*
Golfo de Vizcaya (m) *Bay of Biscay*
goma (f) *rubber band; rubber* (material)
goma de borrar (f) *eraser*
gordo *fat* (adj)
gorra (f) *cap* (hat)
gorro (m) *woollen hat*
gotas (f pl) *drops*
gracias *thank you*
Gran Bretaña *Great Britain*
grande *big, large*
grandes almacenes (m pl) *department store*
granja (f) *farm*
granjero (m) *farmer*
grapadora (f) *stapler*
grasa (f) *fat* (meat etc)
gratis *free* (no charge)
grifo (m) *tap*

gris *grey*
gritar *to shout*
grosellas negras (f pl) *blackcurrants*
grueso *thick*
grupo (m) *party (group)*
guantes (m pl) *gloves*
guapo *attractive, beautiful, handsome (person)*
guerra (f) *war*
guía (m/f) *guide;* **la guía telefónica** *phone book;* **la guía turística** *guide book*
guisantes (m pl) *peas*
guisar *to cook*
guitarra (f) *guitar*
gustar *like:* **me gusta ...** *I like ...;* **me gusta nadar** *I like swimming*

H

habitación (f) *room;* **la habitación doble** *double room;* **la habitación** *individual single room;* **habitaciones libres** *vacancies*
hablar *to talk;* **¿habla ...?** *do you speak ...?;* **no hablo ...** *I don't speak ...*
hacer *to do, make;* **hacer auto-stop** *to hitchhike;* **hacer footing** *to jog;* **hacer punto** *to knit;* **hacer transbordo** *to change (trains etc)* **hace sol** *it's sunny*
hacha (m) *axe*
hacia abajo *down*
hambre *hungry;* **tengo hambre** *I'm hungry*
hamburguesa (f) *hamburger*
hámster (m) *hamster*
harina (f) *flour*
hasta *until*
hay... *there is/are...;* **¿hay ...?** *is/are there ...?*
helado (m) *ice cream*
hepatitis (f) *hepatitis*
herida (f) *injury*
hermana (f) *sister*
hermano (m) *brother*
hervido *boiled*
hervidor de agua (m) *kettle*
hervir *to boil* (water)
hidroaleta (f) *hydrofoil*
hielo (m) *ice*
hierba (f) *grass*
hierro (m) *iron* (material)
hígado (m) *liver*

higo (m) *fig*
hija (f) *daughter*
hijastra (f) *stepdaughter*
hijastro (m) *stepson*
hijo (m) *son*
hincha (m) *football fan*
historia (f) *history*
hobby (m) *hobby*
hoguera (f) *campfire*
hoja (f) *leaf, sheet* (of paper)
hojalata (f) *tin*
hola *hello*
hombre (m) *man*
hombro (m) *shoulder*
homeopatía (f) *homeopathy*
honrado *honest*
hora (f) *hour;* **¿qué hora es?** *what's the time?*
horario (m) *timetable;* **el horario de apertura** *opening times*
horca (f) *garden fork*
horno (m) *oven*
horrible *awful, horrible*
hospital (m) *hospital*
hoy *today*
hueso (m) *bone*
huevo (m) *egg*
húmedo *damp*
humo (m) *smoke*

I

idioma (m) *language*
iglesia (f) *church*
imperdible (m) *safety pin*
imposible *impossible*
impreso de solicitud (m) *application form*
impresora (f) *printer*
incendio (m) *fire (blaze)*
incluido *included*
indigestión (f) *indigestion*
infección (f) *infection*
información (f) *information*
informe (m) *report*
ingeniería (f) *engineering*
Inglaterra *England*
inglés/inglesa *English*
inhalador (m) *inhaler (for asthma etc)*
inmediatamente *immediately*
insecto (m) *insect*
insolación (f) *sunstroke*
insomnio (m) *insomnia*
instrumento musical (m) *musical instrument*
intentar *to try*
interesante *interesting*
intermitente (m) *indicator*

internet (m) *internet*
interpretar *to interpret*
intérprete (m/f) *interpreter*
interruptor (m) *switch*
intoxicación alimenticia (f) *food poisoning*
invitación (f) *invitation*
invitada (f) *guest*
inyección (f) *injection*
ir *to go;* **ir a esquiar** *to go skiing;* **ir de compras** *to go shopping*
Irlanda *Ireland;* **Irlanda del Norte** *Northern Ireland*
irlandés/irlandesa *Irish*
isla (f) *island*
Italia *Italy*
italiano/italiana (m/f) *Italian*
izquierdo *left (not right)*

J

jabón (m) *soap;* **el jabón de lavadora** *washing powder*
jamón (m) *ham*
jarabe (m) *syrup*
jardín (m) *garden*
jarrita (f) *mug*
jarrón (m) *vase*
jaula (f) *cage*
jazz (m) *jazz*
jefe (m) *manager*
jengibre (m) *ginger* (spice)
jerez (m) *sherry*
jeringuilla (f) *syringe*
jersey (m) *sweater*
joven *young*
joyería (f) *jeweller's*
judías (f pl) *beans*
jueves *Thursday*
jugar *to play*
juguete (m) *toy*
julio *July*
junio *June*
junto a *near;* **junto a la puerta** *near the door;* **junto a la ventana** *near the window*
juntos *together*

K, L

kilo (m) *kilo*
kilómetro (m) *kilometre*
kiosko de periódicos (m) *newsagent's*
la (f) *the*
laca (f) *hairspray*
lado de (f) *beside*
ladrón (m) *thief*

lago (m) *lake*
lámpara (f) *lamp*
lamparilla de noche (f) *bedside lamp*
lana (f) *wool*
langosta (f) *lobster*
lápiz (m) *pencil*
largo *long*
las (f pl) *the*
lata (f) *can* (tin)
lavabo (m) *basin* (sink)
lavandería automática (f) *laundrette*
lavavajillas (m) *dishwasher*
laxante (m) *laxative*
leche (f) *milk*; **la leche limpiadora** *cleansing milk* (for skin)
lechuga (f) *lettuce*
leer *to read*
lejía *bleach*
lejos *far, far away*
lengua (f) *tongue*
lente (f) *lens*; **las lentes de contacto** *contact lenses*; **las lentes de contacto semi-rígidas** *gas-permeable lenses*
lento *slow*
letra (f) *letter* (of alphabet)
levantarse *to get up* (rise)
libra (f) *pound* (sterling)
libre *free* (not engaged)
libre de impuestos *duty-free*
libro (m) *book*; **el libro de frases** *phrase book*
licor (m) *liqueur*
ligero *light* (adj: not heavy)
lima (f) *lime* (fruit)
lima de uñas (f) *nailfile*
límite de velocidad (m) *speed limit*
limón (m) *lemon*
limonada (f) *lemonade*
limpio *clean* (adj)
línea (f) *line* (phone etc)
linterna (f) *torch*
lista (f) *list*
listo *clever; ready*
literatura (f) *literature*
litro (m) *litre*
llamar por teléfono *to telephone*
llave (f) *key*; **la llave de las tuercas** *wheel brace*; **la llave inglesa** *wrench*
llegar *to arrive*
lleno *crowded, full*; **estoy lleno** *I'm full* (up)
llorar *to cry* (weep)
lluvia (f) *rain*

lo/la *it*
lo antes posible *as soon as possible*
loción lotion (f); **la loción anti-mosquitos** *insect repellent lotion*; **la loción bronceadora** *suntan lotion*
loco *mad*
lona impermeable (f) *groundsheet*
longitud (f) *length*
los (m pl) *the*
lo siento *I'm sorry*
luces de posición (f pl) *side lights*
lugar (m) *place, sight*; **los lugares de interés de ...** *the sights of ...*
luna (f) *moon*
lunes *Monday*
luz (f) *light*

M

madastra (f) *stepmother*
madera (f) *wood* (material)
madre (f) *mother*
maduro *ripe*
malas hierbas (f pl) *weeds*
maleta (f) *suitcase*
maletero (m) *boot* (car)
Mallorca *Majorca*
malo *bad, poor* (quality)
mama *Mum*
mañana *tomorrow*
mañana (f) *morning*; **por la mañana** *in the morning*
mandar *to send*
mandarina (f) *tangerine*
manga (f) *sleeve*
mano (f) *hand*
manta (f) *blanket, rug*
mantequilla (f) *butter*
manzana (f) *apple*
mapa (m) *map*
maquillaje (m) *make-up*
maquina cortacésped (f) *lawn mower*
máquina de escribir (f) *typewriter*
máquina de fotos (f) *camera*
mar (m) *sea*
marea (f) *tide*
mareado *faint, dizzy*
margarina (f) *margarine*
marido (m) *husband*
mariscos (m pl) *seafood, shellfish*
mármol (m) *marble*
marrón *brown*
Marruecos *Morocco*

martes *Tuesday*
martillo (m) *hammer*
marzo *March*
más *more*; **más de ...** *more than ...*; **más tarde** *later*; **algo más** *something else*; **alguien más** *someone else*
mástil (m) *tent pole*
matrícula (f) *number plate*
mayo *may*
mecánico (m) *mechanic*
media pensión *half board*
medianoche *midnight*
medias (f pl) *tights, stockings*
medicina (f) *medicine*
médico/médica (m/f) *doctor*
medio *half*; **media hora** *half an hour*
mediodía (m) *midday, noon*
Mediterráneo: el Mediterráneo *Mediterranean*
medusa (f) *jellyfish*
mejillones (m pl) *mussels*
mejor *best/better*
melocotón (m) *peach*
melón (m) *melon*
menos *less*
mensaje (m) *message*
mensajería de voz (f) *voicemail*
menú (del día) (m) *set menu*
menudo: a menudo *often*
mercado (m) *market*
mermelada (f) *jam*; **la mermelada de naranja** *marmalade*
mes (m) *month*
mesa (f) *table*; **la mesa de escritorio** *desk*
mesilla de noche (f) *bedside table*
metro (m) *underground* (railway)
mi (s) *my*; **mi libro** *my book*; **mis llaves** *my keys*
microondas (m) *microwave*
miel (f) *honey*
miércoles *Wednesday*
mil *thousand*
minusválido *disabled*
minuto (m) *minute*
mío *mine*; **es míoit's** *mine*
mirar *to watch*
misa (f) *mass* (church)
mismo *same*; **el mismo vestido** *the same dress*; **la misma gente** *the same people*; **lo mismo otra vez, por favor** *same again, please*

mochila (f) *backpack*
moda (f) *fashion*
modem (m) *modem*
mojado *wet*
moneda (f) *coin*
monedero (m) *purse*
monitor (m) *monitor*
montaña (f) *mountain*
monte (m) *hill*
monumento (m) *monument*
morado *purple*
moras (f pl) *blackberries*
mordedura (f) *bite (dog)*
morder *to bite (dog)*
morir *to die*
mosaico (m) *mosaic*
mosca (f) *fly (insect)*
mosquito (m) *mosquito*
mostaza (f) *mustard*
mostrador (m) *worktop;* **el mostrador de facturación** *check-in desk*
motocicleta (f) *motorcycle*
motor (m) *engine (motor)*
motora (f) *motorboat*
mover *to move (something);* **moverse** *move oneself;* **¡no se mueva!** *don't move!*
mucho *much/many, a lot;* **mucho mejor** *much better;* **mucho más despacio** *much slower;* **no muchos** *not many*
mudarse *(de casa) to move (house)*
muebles (m pl) *furniture*
muela (f) *back tooth*
muelle (m) *dock; spring (mechanical)*
muerto *dead*
mujer (f) *woman, wife*
muletas (f pl) *crutches*
muñeca (f) *wrist*
muro (m) *wall (outside)*
museo (m) *museum*
música (f) *music;* **la música clásica** *classical music;* **la música folklórica** *folk music;* **la música pop** *pop music*
músico (m) *musician*
muy *very*

N

nací en ... *I was born in ...*
nada *nothing;* **no queda nada** *there's nothing left;* **no sirve de nada** *it's no use*
nadar *to swim*

nadie *nobody*
naranja (f) *orange (fruit);* *orange (adj)*
nariz (f) *nose*
nata (f) *cream (dairy)*
natación (f) *swimming*
náuseas *sick;* **tengo náuseas** *I feel sick*
navaja (f) *penknife*
navidad (f) *Christmas*
necesario *necessary*
necesito ... *I need ...*
negar *to deny*
negativo (m) *negative (photo)*
negocio (m) *business*
negro *black*
neozelandés/ neozelandesa *New Zealander*
neumático (m) *tyre*
ni ... ni ... *neither ... nor ...*
niebla (f) *fog*
nieta (f) *granddaughter*
nieto (m) *grandson*
nieve (f) *snow*
ninguno/ninguna: ninguno de ellos *neither of them;* **en ninguna parte** *nowhere*
niño/niña *child (m/f);* **los niños** *children;* **el niño pequeño** *baby*
no *no (response), not;* **no hay de qué** *you're welcome; no* **importa** *it doesn't matter;* **no es/está ...** (s) *he's not ...*
noche (f) *night*
nombre (m) *name;* **el nombre de pila** *first name*
norte (m) *north*
nosotros/nosotras *we, us;* **es para nosotros/ nosotras** *it's for us*
noticias (f pl) *news*
novela (f) *novel*
noventa *ninety*
novia (f) *girlfriend*
noviembre *November*
novio (m) *boyfriend*
nudista (m/f) *nudist*
nuestro *our;* **es nuestro** *it's ours*
Nueva Zelanda *New Zealand*
nueve *nine*
nuevo *new*
nuez (f) *nut (fruit)*
número (m) *number;* **los números** *figures*
nunca *never*

O

o *or;* **o bien ... o ...** *either ... or ...*
obra de teatro (f) *play (theatre)*
obturador (m) *shutter (camera)*
Océano Atlántico (m) *Atlantic Ocean*
ochenta *eighty*
ocho *eight*
octubre *October*
oculista (m/f) *optician*
ocupado *busy (engaged); occupied*
oeste (m) *west*
oficina (f) *office (place); branch (of company);* **la oficina de objetos perdidos** *lost property office;* **la oficina de turismo** *tourist office*
oído (m) *(inner) ear*
¡oiga, por favor! *excuse me! (to get attention); waiter/waitress!*
oír *to hear*
ojo (m) *eye*
ola (f) *wave*
oler *to smell*
olivo (m) *olive tree*
olor (m) *smell*
oloroso *sweet (sherry)*
olvidar *to forget*
once *eleven*
ondulado *wavy (hair)*
operación (f) *operation*
operadora (f) *operator*
oporto (m) *port (drink)*
orden del día (m) *agenda*
ordenador (m) *computer*
oreja *ear* (f)
órgano (m) *organ (music)*
oro (m) *gold*
orquesta (f) *orchestra*
oscuro *dark;* **azul oscuro** *dark blue*
ostra (f) *oyster*
otra vez *again*
otro *another; other;* **el otro** *the other one;* **en otro sitio** *somewhere else*

P

padastro (m) *stepfather*
padre (m) *father;* **los padres** *parents*
pagar *to pay;* **pagar al contado** *to pay cash*

página (f) *page*

pago (m) *payment*

país (m) *country (state)*

pájaro (m) *bird*

pala (f) *spade*

palabra (f) *word*

palacio (m) *palace*

palanca de velocidades (f) *gear stick*

pálido *pale*

pan (m) *bread*

panadería (f) *bakery*

pañal (m) *nappy;* **los pañales desechables** *disposable nappies*

paño de cocina (m) *dish cloth*

pantalla (f) *lampshade, screen*

pantalón (m) *trousers;* **los pantalones cortos** *shorts*

pantis (m pl) *tights*

pañuelo (m) *headscarf;* **los pañuelos de papel** *tissues*

papá *dad*

papel (m) *paper;* **el papel de envolver/regalo** *wrapping paper;* **el papel de escribir** *writing paper;* **el papel higiénico** *toilet paper;* **los papeles de filtro** *filter papers*

paquete (m) *package, packet, parcel*

par (m) *pair*

para *for; es para mí it's for me;* **para el viernes** *by Friday;* **¿para qué?** *what for?;* **para una semana** *for a week*

parabrisas (m) *windscreen*

parachoques (m) *bumper*

parada (f) *stop (bus);* **la parada de taxis** *taxi rank*

parafina (f) *paraffin*

paraguas (m) *umbrella*

parar *to stop*

pared (f) *wall (inside)*

pariente (m) *relative*

parque (m) *park*

parrilla (f) *grill*

parte de atrás (f) *back (not front)*

parterre (m) *flowerbed*

partido (m) *match (sport); party (political)*

pasajero (m) *passenger*

pasaporte (m) *passport;* **el pasaporte de animales** *pet passport*

pasas (f pl) *raisins*

paseo (m) *walk, stroll;* **ir de**

paseo *to go for a walk*

pasillo (m) *aisle, corridor*

paso elevado (m) *flyover*

pasta (f) *pasta*

pasta dentífrica (f) *toothpaste*

pastel (m) *cake (small)*

pastelería (f) *cake shop*

pastilla (f) *pill, tablet;* **las pastillas de menta** *peppermints;* **las pastillas para la garganta** *cough drops*

patata (f) *potato;* **las patatas fritas** *chips, crisps*

patinar *to skid*

patines *para* **hielo** (m pl) *ice skates*

peatón (m) *pedestrian*

pecho (m) *chest (part of body)*

pedazo (m) *piece*

pedido (m) *order*

pegamento (m) *adhesive, glue*

peinar *to comb*

peine (m) *comb*

película (f) *film, movie;* **la película en color** *colour film*

peligroso *dangerous*

pelo (m) *hair*

pelota (f) *ball*

peluquería (f) *hairdresser;* **la peluquería de caballeros** *barber*

pendientes (m pl) *earrings*

pensar *to think;* **lo pensaré** *I'll think about it*

pensión completa *full board*

peor *worse, worst*

pepino (m) *cucumber*

pequeño *little, small*

pera (f) *pear*

percha (f) *coat hanger*

¡perdón! *sorry!, excuse me! (when sneezing etc)*

perejil (m) *parsley*

perezoso *lazy*

perfecto *perfect*

perfume (m) *perfume*

periódico (m) *newspaper*

perla (f) *pearl*

permanente (f) *perm*

permiso (m) *licence*

pero *but*

perro (m) *dog*

persianas (f pl) *blinds*

pesado *heavy*

pesca (f) *fishing*

pescadería (f) *fishmonger's*

pescado (m) *fish (food)*

pescar: ir a pescar *to go fishing*

pez (m) *fish (animal)*

piano (m) *piano*

picadura (f) *bite (by insect)*

picaporte (m) *handle (door)*

picar *to bite (insect)*

picas (f pl) *spades (cards)*

picnic (m) *picnic*

pie (m) *foot*

pierna (f) *leg*

pijama (m) *pyjamas*

pila (f) *battery (torch etc)*

piloto (m) *pilot*

pimienta (f) *pepper (spice)*

pimiento (m) *pepper (red, green)*

pin (m) *PIN*

piña (f) *pineapple*

pinchazo (m) *puncture*

pino (m) *pine (tree)*

pintor (m) *decorator*

pintura (f) *paint*

pinza (f) *peg;* **las pinzas** *tweezers*

pipa (f) *pipe (for smoking)*

Pirineos: los Pirineos *Pyrenees*

piscina (f) *swimming pool;* **la piscina municipal** *public swimming pool*

piso (m) *apartment; floor (storey)*

pista (f) *runway*

pistola (f) *gun (pistol)*

piston (m) *piston*

pizza (f) *pizza*

plancha (f) *iron (for clothes);* **a la plancha** *grilled*

planchar *to iron*

plano (m) *town map, town plan; (adj) flat, level*

planta (f) *plant*

planta baja (f) *ground floor*

plástico (m) *plastic;* **el plástico para envolver** *plastic wrap*

plata (f) *silver (metal)*

plátano (m) *banana*

plateado *silver (colour)*

platillo (m) *saucer*

plato (m) *plate;* **el plato principal** *main course;* **los platos preparados** *ready meals*

playa (f) *beach*

plaza (f) *pitch, square (in town);* **la plaza de toros** *bullring*

pluma (f) *pen;* **la pluma estilográfica** *fountain pen*

pobre *poor (not rich)*

poco *a little;* **poco común** *unusual;* **poco hecho/ pasado** *rare (steak)*
poder *to be able*
policía (f) *police*
policía (m) *police officer*
política (f) *politics*
pollo (m) *chicken*
polvo (m) *powder;* **los polvos** *make-up powder;* **los polvos de talco** *talcum powder*
pomada (f) *ointment*
poner *to put;* **¿me pone ...?** *can I have ...?*
poquito *a little;* **sólo un poquito** *just a little*
por *through, by, per;* **por avión** *by air mail;* **por la noche** *at night;* **por noche** *per night;* **por todas partes** *everywhere*
porcelana (f) *china (wear)*
por favor *please*
¿por qué? *why?*
porque *because*
portero (m) *caretaker*
Portugal *Portugal*
portugués *Portuguese*
posible *possible*
postal (f) *postcard*
póster (m) *poster*
postigo (m) *shutter (window)*
postre (m) *dessert*
precio (m) *price;* **el precio de entrada** (m) *admission charge*
precioso *beautiful (object)*
preferir *to prefer*
pregunta (f) *question*
presupuesto (m) *budget, estimate*
primavera (f) *spring (season)*
primer piso (m) *first floor*
primero *first;* **de primera** *first class;* **primeros auxilios** *first aid*
primo (m) *cousin*
prima (f) *cousin*
principiante (m/f) *beginner*
principio (m) *start, beginning*
prisa: tengo prisa *I'm in a hurry*
privado *private*
problema (m) *problem*
producto (m) *product;* **los productos de belleza** *beauty products;* **los productos del hogar** *household products;* **los productos lácteos** *dairy products*

profesión (f) *profession*
profesor/profesora (m/f) *teacher*
profesor/profesora de universidad (m/f) *lecturer (university)*
profundo *deep*
programa (m) *schedule*
prohibido *prohibited*
prometida (f) *fiancée*
prometido (m) *fiancé*
prometido/prometida (m/f) *engaged (to be married)*
propina (f) *tip (money)*
próximo *next*
prudente *careful*
prueba (f) *test*
público *public*
pueblo (m) *small town, village*
¿puede ...? *can you ...?*
puedo *I can;* **no puedo** *I can't*
puente (m) *bridge*
puerta (f) *door, gate;* **la puerta de embarque** *departure gate*
puerto (m) *harbour, port*
pulga (f) *flea*
pulpo (m) *octopus*
pulsera (f) *bracelet*
punta (f) *tip (end)*
puro (m) *cigar*

Q

que *than*
¿qué? *what?*
quemadura (f) *burn*
quemadura de sol (f) *sunburn*
quemar *to burn*
querer *to want, love*
querido *dear (person)*
queso (m) *cheese*
¿qué tal? *how are you?*
¿quién? *who?*
quinze *fifteen*
quirófano (m) *operating theatre*
quisquillas (f pl) *shrimps*
quizás *maybe, perhaps*

R

rábano (m) *radish*
radiador (m) *radiator*
radio (f) *radio*
rápido *fast, quick*
raro *rare (uncommon)*
rastrillo (m) *rake*
rata (f) *rat*
ratón (m) *mouse*

raya (f) *parting (hair)*
rebajas (f pl) *sale (at reduced prices)*
rebeca (f) *cardigan*
recado (m) *message*
recepción (f) *reception*
recepcionista (m/f) *receptionist*
receta (f) *prescription*
recibo (m) *receipt*
recobrar algo *to get something back*
recogida (f) *collection (postal)*
récord (m) *record (sport etc)*
recuerdo (m) *souvenir*
redondo *round (circular)*
regalo (m) *gift;* **el regalo de cumpleaños** *birthday present*
regla (f) *ruler (for measuring)*
reír *to laugh*
rejilla de equipajes (f) *luggage rack*
relajarse *to relax*
religión (f) *religion*
relleno (m) *filling (in sandwich, cake)*
reloj (m) *clock, watch*
remar *to row*
remolque (m) *trailer*
remos (m pl) *oars*
resaca (f) *hangover*
reserva (f) *reservation*
reservar *to book*
resfriado (m) *cold (illness);* **tengo un resfriado** *I have a cold*
respirar *to breathe*
restaurante (m) *restaurant*
resto (m) *rest, remainder*
retrasado *delayed;* **el autobús se ha retrasado** *the bus is late*
reunión (f) *meeting*
revelar *to develop (film)*
revista (f) *magazine*
rico *rich*
rímel (m) *mascara*
rincón (m) *corner (of room)*
riñón (m) *kidney*
río (m) *river*
rizos (m pl) *curls*
robar *steal;* **lo han robado** *it's been stolen*
robo (m) *robbery*
roca (f) *rock (stone)*
rock (m) *rock (music)*
rodilla (f) *knee*
rojo *red*
ron (m) *rum*

ropa (f) *clothes*; **la ropa de cama** (f) *bed linen*; **la ropa interior** *underwear*; **la ropa sucia** *laundry (dirty)*
rosa (adj) *pink*
rosa (f) *rose*
roto *broken*
rotonda (f) *roundabout*
rotulador (m) *felt-tip pen*
roulotte (f) *caravan*
rubí (m) *ruby (stone)*
rubio *blond(e)* (adj)
rueda (f) *wheel*; **la rueda pinchada** *flat tyre*
rugby (m) *rugby*
ruidoso *noisy*
ruinas (f pl) *ruins*
rulos (m pl) *curlers*

S

sábado *Saturday*
sábana (f) *sheet (bedding)*
saber *to know (fact)*; **no sé** *I don't know*
sabor (m) *flavour*
sacacorchos (m) *corkscrew*
sacapuntas (m) *pencil sharpener*
sacar *to bring out*
saco de dormir (m) *sleeping bag*
sal (f) *salt*
sala de espera (f) *waiting room*
sala de pediatría (f) *children's ward*
salchicha (f) *sausage*
salida (f) *exit, departure*; **las salidas** *departures*; **la salida de emergencia** *emergency exit*
salmón (m) *salmon*
salón (m) *lounge (in hotel)*
salsa (f) *sauce*
¡salud! *cheers! (toast)*
sandalias (f pl) *sandals*
sangre (f) *blood*
sartén (f) *frying pan*
sauna (f) *sauna*
secador (de pelo) (m) *hairdryer*
seco *dry*
sed *thirsty*; **tengo sed** *I'm thirsty*
seda (f) *silk*
segundo (m) *second* (noun; adj); **de segunda** *second class*
seguro (m) *insurance*; (adj) *sure, safe (not dangerous)*
seis *six*

sello (m) *stamp*
selva *rainforest*
semáforo (m) *traffic lights*
semana (f) *week*; **la semana pasada** *last week*; **la semana que viene** *next week*
seminario (m) *seminar*
semi-seco *medium-dry (wine)*
señal (f) *deposit*
sencillo *simple*
senderismo (m) *hiking*
señor *Mr, sir*
señora *Mrs, madam*
señorita *Miss*
separado *separated*
septiembre *September*
ser *to be*
serio *serious*
seropositivo *HIV positive*
servicio (m) *service, department*; **el servicio de habitaciones** *room service*; **el servicio de radiología** *x-ray department*; **el servicio de urgencias** *emergency department*
servicios (m pl) *toilets (in public establishment)*; **los servicios de caballeros** *men's toilets*; **los servicios de señoras** *women's toilets*
servilleta (f) *napkin*
sesenta *sixty*
setas (f pl) *mushrooms*
setenta *seventy*
seto (m) *hedge*
si *if, whether*
sí *yes*
Sida (m) *AIDS*
siempre *always*
siete *seven*
significar: **¿qué significa esto?** *what does this mean?*
siguiente *next*
silla (f) *chair*; **la silla de ruedas** *wheelchair*
sillita de ruedas (f) *stroller, pushchair*
simpático *friendly*
sin *without*; **sin plomo** *unleaded*
sinagoga (f) *synagogue*
sitio (m) *room, space*; **el sitio web** *website*
sobre (m) *envelope*
sobre todo *especially*
sobrina (f) *niece*
sobrino (m) *nephew*
soda (f) *soda water*

sofa (m) *sofa*
sofocante *close, stuffy*
sol (m) *sun*
solo *alone*; **yo solo** *by myself*
sólo *just, only*
soltero/soltera (m/f) *single (unmarried)*
solución limpiadora (f) *soaking solution (for contact lenses)*
sombrero (m) *hat*
sombrilla (f) *sunshade*
somnífero (m) *sleeping pill*
somos *we are*
son *they are*
sonreír *to smile*
sonrisa (f) *smile*
sopa (f) *soup*
sordo *deaf*
sostén (m) *bra*
sótano (m) *basement*
soy *I am*; **soy de ...** *I come from ...*
spray (m) *inhaler (for asthma etc)*; **el spray antipulgas** *flea spray*
su (s) *its/hers/his/your (formal)*; **¿es suyo esto?** *is this yours?*
subirse *to get in, get on (of train, bus etc)*
sucio *dirty*
sudadera (f) *sweatshirt*
Sudamérica *South America*
sudar *to sweat*
sudor (m) *sweat*
suelo (m) *floor*; **el suelo aislante** *groundsheet*
sueño (m) *sleep*
suerte (f) *luck*; **¡suerte!** *good luck!*
supermercado (m) *supermarket*
suplemento (m) *supplement*
supositorio (m) *suppository*
sur (m) *south*

T

tabaco (m) *tobacco*
tabla de windsurfing (f) *sailboard*
tableta de chocolate (f) *bar of chocolate*
tacón (m) *heel (shoe)*
taller (m) *garage (for repairs)*
talón (m) *heel (foot)*
talonario de cheques (m) *chequebook*
también *too (also)*
tampones (m pl) *tampons*

tan so; **tan bueno** so good
tanto: no tanto not so much; **tanto ... como ...** both ... and ...
tapiz (m) tapestry
tapón (m) cap (bottle), plug (sink)
taquilla (f) box office, ticket office
tarde (f) evening; (adj) late; it's getting late **se está haciendo** tarde
tarifa (f) fare
tarjeta (f) card; **la tarjeta de banco** bank card; **la tarjeta de crédito** credit card; **la tarjeta de embarque** boarding pass; **la tarjeta de vista** business card; **la tarjeta telefónica** phonecard
tarta (f) cake (large)
taxi (m) taxi
taza (f) cup
té (m) tea
techo (m) ceiling
teclado (m) keyboard
técnico (m) technician
tejado (m) roof
tejanos (m pl) jeans
tela (f) material (cloth)
teleférico (m) cable car
teléfono (m) telephone; el **teléfono móvil** mobile phone
televisión (f) television; la **television por** cable cable TV
temperatura (f) temperature
temprano early
tenedor (m) fork
tener to have; **tengo** I have; **no tengo** I don't have; **¿tiene?** do you have?; **tengo que irme** I have to go; **tengo calor** I feel hot; **tengo que ...** I must ...
teñir to bleach (hair)
tenis (m) tennis
tenue faint (unclear)
tercero third
terminal (f) terminal
ternera (f) veal
terraza (f) terrace
testigo (m) witness
tía (f) aunt
tiempo (m) time, weather
tienda (f) shop; **la tienda de comestibles** grocer's; la **tienda de discos** record store
tienda (de campaña) (f) tent

¿tiene ...? do you have ...?
tierra (f) land, soil
tijeras (f pl) scissors
timbre (m) bell (door)
tinta (f) ink
tinto red (wine)
tintorería (f) dry cleaner
tío (m) uncle
tirantes (m pl) braces
tirar de to pull
tirita (f) plaster
toalla (f) towel
toallitas para bebé (f pl) baby wipes
tobillo (m) ankle
toca: me toca a mí it's my turn
tocadiscos (m) record player
tocar to feel (touch)
todavía yet; todavía no not yet
todo everything, all; **eso es todo** that's all
todos everyone
todos los días every day
tomar to take; **tomar el sol** to sunbathe
tomate (m) tomato
tónica (f) tonic
torero (m) bullfighter
tormenta (f) storm
tornillo (m) screw
toro (m) bull
torre (f) tower
tortilla (f) omelette
tos (f) cough
toser to cough
tostada (f) toast
trabajar to work (job)
trabajo (m) job, work
tractor (m) tractor
tradición (f) tradition
traducir to translate
traductor/traductora (m/f) translator
traer to fetch
tráfico (m) traffic
traje (m) suit (clothing)
tranquilo quiet
trapo del polvo (m) duster
trasero (m) bottom (part of body)
tréboles (m pl) clubs (cards)
trece thirteen
treinta thirty
tren (m) train
tres three
triste sad
tú you (informal)

tu (s) your (informal); **tu libro** your book; **tus zapatos** your shoes; **¿es tuyo esto?** is this yours?
tubería (f) pipe (for water)
tubo de escape (m) exhaust
tuerca (f) nut (for bolt)
tuerza (a la izquierda/derecha) turn (left/right)
túnel (m) tunnel
turismo (m) sightseeing
turista (m/f) tourist

U

último last (final)
ultramarinos (m) grocer
un/una a
uña (f) finger nail
único single (only)
universidad (f) university
uno one
urgente urgent
usar to use
uso (m) use
usted you (formal)
utensilios de cocina (m pl) cooking utensils
útil useful
uvas (f pl) grapes

V

vacaciones (f pl) holiday
vacío empty
vacuna (f) vaccination
vagón (m) carriage (train); **el vagón-restaurante** restaurant car
vainilla (f) vanilla
vale OK
valle (m) valley
válvula (f) valve
vapor (m) steam, steamer (boat); **al vapor** steamed
vaqueros (m pl) jeans
varios several
vaso (m) glass (for drinking)
váter (m) toilet (item in bathroom)
¡váyase! go away!
veces: a veces sometimes
vegetariano vegetarian
vehículo (m) vehicle
veinte twenty
vela (f) sailing; candle
velocidad (f) speed
venda (f) bandage